Elegantly FRUGAL COSTUMES

The poor man's do-it-yourself costume maker's guide

by

EY
NG

by
SON

ING, LTD.
olorado

Meriwether Publishing Ltd., Publisher
Box 7710
Colorado Springs, CO 80933

Editors: Arthur L. Zapel, Pat Middleton
Typesetting: Sharon E. Garlock
Art direction: Tom Myers
Cover design: Michelle Gallardo, Tom Myers, Beth Tallakson
Interior illustrations: Beth Tallakson

© Copyright MCMXCII Meriwether Publishing Ltd.
Printed in the United States of America
First Edition

Library of Congress Cataloging-in-Publication Data

Dearing, Shirley, 1931-
    Elegantly frugal costumes! : the poor man's do-it-yourself costume maker's guide / by Shirley Dearing; illustrated by Beth Tallakson. : 1st ed.
      p.   cm.
    ISBN 0-916260-88-7 : $10.95
    1. Costume. 2. Costume design. I. Title.
TT649.D4 1992
646.4'78--dc20
                                        92-1662
                                        CIP

DEDICATION

*To Karen Onufrock, who proved to me that
I, too, could make a tailcoat.*

To J. Julius Baird, who was never afraid of new ways.

*To my husband, on whose imagination
I could count on when mine failed.*

ACKNOWLEDGMENT

The author wishes to express her appreciation to Pat Middleton for her extensive work and counsel in editing and finalizing the original manuscript for publication.

CONTENTS

INTRODUCTION

In the fourth grade play, you were one of six Pilgrims. Your cousin Joe was an Indian. Three years ago, you and your husband went to the Christmas costume ball as Romeo and Juliet. Rare is the person who at one time or another hasn't been called upon to wear a costume — or provide one for someone else.

While we all enjoy the splendor that is Hollywood, extravagant costumes are not something most community theaters or elementary schools can afford. In fact, many mothers have stretched their imaginations to new limits making goats and shepherds out of third graders!

When I first began making costumes, I bought the material and made each one from scratch, not realizing there were fortunes in time, effort, and money to be saved with just a little ingenuity. The experienced eye looks at a black princess-style coat and sees it trimmed to reflect a style popular in the early 1800s. Children's costumes need not be constructed from collar to hem when an old dress could be transformed with only a primitive bit of sewing, or a lady's blouse might very nicely antique a young boy. Even those who sew constantly don't naturally think in these metamorphic terms, because it isn't relevant to everyday sewing. Knowing how to sew gives you an advantage, but you don't have to be an expert to assemble a costume that begins with a fitted bodice from a discarded dress or that is built on an old coat.

In this book I hope to share with you some ideas that have proven effective for me: some shortcuts that will save you time, money, and headaches. A limited budget doesn't mean you can't have elegant costumes — frugality doesn't mean you must sacrifice the excitement that costumes bring to the stage. The concept is the key . . . and a little imagination!

Shirley Dearing

1

Chapter 1
RESOURCES: WHERE DO I START?

To Be or Not to Be Authentic

To be authentic, according to Webster, is to be genuine and real. The costumer who gets hung up on authenticity spends too much money and time on a job that's of no lasting worth. Besides, costumes are usually associated with fun, and it's a shame to spoil that fun by establishing unrealistic goals. From a practical standpoint, few theater companies can afford authentic costumes — and few collectors would part with them! — so we must strive for authentic effect. That is, we must carefully research the clothing of the time period, then achieve a look that will imitate reality for our audience (who, by the way, seldom sees your costumes in the same light or from the same distance that you do).

The Research of Others

Your job should begin at your local library. Remember, it's unlikely you're doing anything that hasn't been done before, and chances are someone else has done much of the research for you.

Historic Costume for the Stage by Lucy Barton will provide you with a wealth of information. Besides including many different categories of costumes, such as equestrian and military, she also tells you a lot about costume construction.

What People Wore by Douglas Gorsline is one of the broader collections if you're interested in ordinary people rather than just the upper classes, though there is seldom enough about ordinary costuming in any one book.

The Mode in Costume by R. Turner Wilcox has pictures that show a great deal of detail.

Millia Davenport's *Book of Costume* is best for decorative effects and ways of trimming, since it contains a large collection of paintings.

In *A History of Costume,* Carl Kohler supplies actual patterns you can enlarge. It's always helpful to see how a particular piece of a garment is shaped.

Janet Arnold's *Patterns of Fashion 1860-1940* is a collection of authentic patterns, which is especially handy for getting an idea of how the complicated clothes of late Victorian times were draped. This book will probably not be in a library, but it can be ordered from Hobby Horse Press, 416 Ben Franklin Station, Washington, DC 20044. If you're working with late 19th-century costumes, it's worth the trouble.

Pictorial Encyclopedia of Fashion is another good collection of paintings and is good for accessories.

For military costume, Preben Kannik's little book *Military Uniforms of the World in Color* is good.

Sketch Book '76 will show you the shape of all sorts of things used during the American Revolution. (R. L. Klinger, 4505 N. 20th St., Arlington, VA 22207.)

There are quite a few books on peasant costume, and *Peasant Costume in Europe* by Kathleen Mann is probably as good as any, but it is limited to what I call "festival" costuming: Sunday clothes, not what people who lived off the land wore every day. Art history books are another good source, especially for the middle and lower classes. Two specifically come to mind: *17th & 18th Century Art* by Julius S. Held and Donald Posner, and *History of Renaissance Art* by Frederick Hartt.

There are a surprising number of costume books but once you have become familiar with a few, you will begin to notice that many of them feature photographs of the same paintings.

While all of these books are full of wonderful infor-

4

mation, they are not necessarily conveniently organized; not if all you want to find out about is a final touch such as shoes, hats, or some other accessory. For this you might have to hunt through several chapters or even several different volumes. For convenience, I have culled some of the most basic accessories and organized them chronologically. It should be possible, for instance, to look under each period in this book's table of contents for "headgear" and find a page reference for at least one style for each period.

Trash to Treasure: Discards and Donations

Whether you're a parent costuming your child for the Christmas play, or the costumer of a large production, the best way to save money is to use your imagination. With a big budget, making beautiful costumes is relatively easy. You can afford material that is beautiful in itself, and you can afford people who can sew and fit. The less money you have to spend, the more you will have to improvise as you learn how to see things in a new way and how to make something out of nothing.

Your treasure hunt should begin in the closets in your own home, whether your goal is one specific costume or an entire wardrobe. Remember that you may embellish a simple skirt, or shirt, or you may dissect it to use only parts to create something entirely different.

If you're likely to be in the costuming business (either as an employee or a volunteer), get into the habit of checking the thrift shops, flea markets, church bazaars, rummage sales, and garage sales for old clothing. If you're really lucky, you might pick something up that's authentic. At worst, you could find some piece that would lend itself to transformation, often at a very reasonable price. Don't wait for a need to arise; if you see something appropriate for another time period or character, pick it up. Maybe next season it will be just what you're looking for!

Thrift shops run by organizations that have volunteer help, like churches, will probably be cheaper than the Salvation Army or Goodwill. In our town there is a church with a particularly well-to-do congregation, and the thrift shop it runs offers designer clothes at incredibly low prices. Many gowns are easily transformed into elegant costumes; gowns of gorgeous material, with all sorts of marvelous decoration already in place. Occasionally, I have found gowns that were perfect just as they were, or with the simple addition of a new sleeve.

A good thrift shop will have an unlimited supply of accessories. Shoes are the most outstanding; after that, jewelry, hats, underwear, and stockings. It's mostly a matter of training your eye. There's no reason for a 19th-century character to wear chunky heels just because that's all you can buy now. Shoes with little heels still turn up in thrift shops regularly. Keep in mind that clothes and shoes come back in cycles. Five years ago, you couldn't have found a pair of plaid pants anywhere. Now they're beginning to creep into thrift shop shelves. In a year, there'll be a deluge. Remember the fancy shirts of the late '60s? And how about the clogs now . . . just great for peasants (that's what they wore for several hundred years).

"It pays to advertise" is an axiom familiar to business but true in costuming as well. If you need clothing from the 1920s, someone's grandmother may be happy to spend an hour with you in her attic going through an old trunk. You'll probably listen to some terrific stories, and you may come away with authentic costumes that will bring real life and energy to your stage! But you'll have to get the word out in a public way: an ad in the local paper, a notice posted on the bulletin board at the grocery store, an announcement made at the PTA meeting. A word of caution: Don't take clothing or props on loan with the promise of returning them. If someone isn't willing to donate the item you need, don't borrow it. Too often an unavoidable accident leads to hurt feelings — or worse. Of course, if you're working with a nonprofit group, remember that you may motivate patrons to donate items by furnishing receipts for tax purposes.

A guild or auxiliary of some sort can be a tremendous

6

help to a costumer. Though you probably won't have time to work on the various projects the auxiliary becomes involved in, don't make the mistake of thinking you're too busy to attend meetings and get to know the people who are interested in helping your company. Your time will be repaid twofold, and you'll meet some nice people who will become your most understanding friends and your greatest supporters.

Before I began my campaign for hand-me-downs and second-hand fabric, I discussed it with our company manager. Would begging for cast-offs put the company in a bad light? Wisely, he said no, he didn't think so, since most people preferred to think of management as being frugal rather than extravagant. And our opera guild reacted in just that way. Very soon there was a nucleus of people who made every effort to supply me with things I asked for, and who made a point of never throwing anything away without first asking if I could use it.

Availability and interest within any group will vary. In the early years of our guild there were quite a few women who could sew and who wanted to help make costumes. As the years went by the guild's own projects expanded: large parties, festivals, and so on. Nevertheless, there will always be supporters for whom it is easier to give goods and service than cash.

Often when an estate is being settled, a residue of things that no one knows what to do with remains. I have "inherited" Victorian jet, paisley shawls, fans, laces, feathers, old dresses, and quite a few tail coats. (You may notice that our great-grandparents were significantly smaller than we are today. Some of those authentic dresses or tails are too small to be used for anything other than examples.) If you can collect enough authentic clothing, you might consider a fashion show as a method of increasing awareness of your production or raising money to improve the costumes you really need.

7

Fabulous Fabrics: Draperies Don't Just Dress Windows

Ever since a desperate Scarlett O'Hara needed something special to wear for Rhett, draperies have been providing material for leading ladies. Remember the von Trapp children when Maria replaced their uniforms with clothing suitable for frolicking? Draperies. They come in marvelous textures and luxurious lengths. Brocades, velvets, tapestries, and even small prints have much more character than plain fabric. Even patterns that are large or loud can be useful after a dye job. Of course, dyeing a fabric demands that it be ironed. Don't delude yourself — wrinkles do show. Stage lighting may do wonders for washed-out stains, but wrinkles will be accentuated. A clean, crisp look is very important, so ironing will always be with us. Spray starch is your dearest friend, allowing you to freshen the most bedraggled heirloom.

A bonus that often comes with drapery is the lining. For a dress with lots of body and fullness, I cut the lining right along with the fabric. Drapery fabric with contemporary patterns too strong to be dyed out makes excellent lining or underskirts. Bedspreads, tablecloths, sheets — just about anything with yardage — the possibilities are limited only by your imagination!

I have been given many yards of fabric that my company would never have been able to buy: antique silk velvets from France, Italian brocade, and more. Besides being beautiful and rich, these fabrics are also unique which makes the costumes you create so much more interesting and original. The same principle applies to many of the gowns you receive or find in thrift shops. After working with old treasures, it's a let-down to see costumes made of cheap materials, even if they're brand new. The kind of new materials the average community company can afford will look very cheap by comparison.

Chapter 2
Period Costumes

Biblical to Medieval

The tunic — simple to make, easy to care for, and guaranteed to be in style for hundreds of years for beggars and kings and everyone in between. Short tunics, long tunics, tunics in layers: The tunic was the basic costume from pre-biblical times all the way up to the Renaissance. Younger people and people who lived in warmer climates wore shorter ones and fewer layers. Colder climates and advanced age demanded longer ones and more layers. But everyone wore tunics.

Fabric and quantity denoted affluence. Wealthy people had richer, more colorful fabrics and a selection of garments. They frequently wore a square-cut robe with full sleeves over their tunics. Garments worn by the poor were likely made of homespun, coarse fabric died brown or tan because these were the most common dyes. The poor often wore their one garment night and day until it wore out.

To make a tunic for a small to middle-sized shepherd, try to find something on the order of a coarse, woven Mexican shirt. In a pinch, a regular shirt will do. (See figures 2.1 and 2.2 on page 10.)

- Cut off the hem. (Don't waste time ripping.)
- Cut off the sleeves.
- Cut off the hood.
- Use fabric from the sleeves or the hood to add desired length (about down to the knees).

Raggedness is probably appropriate, but if you want a more finished look, you can hem or trim with bands of fabric. A sash can be anything: a cord or a piece of the same material. Your oldest, dingiest, heaviest fabrics will work well for both this smock and this tunic. (See figures 2.3 on page 11 and 2.4 on page 12.)

Figure 2.1 – Contemporary coarse-woven Mexican shirt

Figure 2.2 – Tunic

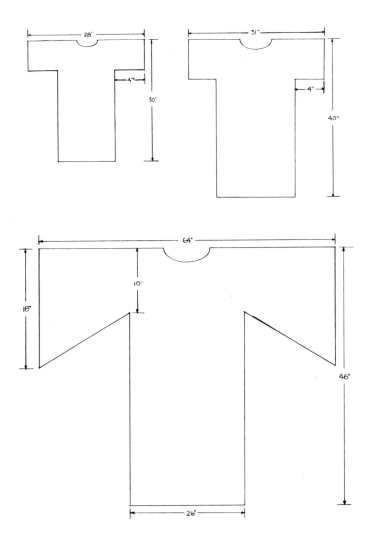

Figure 2.3 – Patterns for tunics

11

Figure 2.4 – Smock

If your fabric looks too clean, a dunking in dark dye will muddy it, along with little or no ironing. Peasants working in the fields did not wear crisp, bright clothing. A few holes and rips are even appropriate.

To make an elegant peasant shirt, use a regular white shirt. Remove the collar and add full sleeves with trim. (See figure 2.5 on page 13.)

Figure 2.5 – Elegant peasant shirt

A nightgown (be careful of pinks and blues — too much of a bedroom look) can often be used for a tunic. You might find evening dresses that are tunic-style and made of rich fabric. Be sure to check the maternity department at the thrift store for straight-cut dresses or dresses with elastic at the waist that can be removed. Sheets, bedspreads and brocade curtains make wonderful tunics and robes.

Garments to be worn over a tunic can be made from shirts, too, or from sweaters. Cut off the ribbing and cut down the front so that it's like a vest. Vests can be long or short. A robe was frequently worn over the tunic by kings and other nobility. These were the same shape as a kimono bathrobe. (This is sometimes referred to as "bathrobe costuming.") Bathrobes can, indeed, be quite suitable. If you have to make one, kimono patterns are available. (See figure 2.6.)

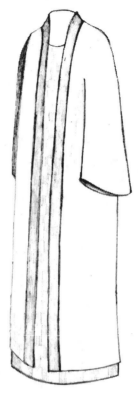

Figure 2.6 – Robe

A mantle is another garment to be worn over a tunic. A simple piece of cloth which wraps around the body for warmth and elegance, it should be three to four feet wide and long enough to reach the ankles of the person who will be wearing it. A mantle can be fastened over one shoulder or over both shoulders and fastened under the chin. It may also be slung over a shoulder and wrapped around the waist. (See figure 2.27 on page 15.)

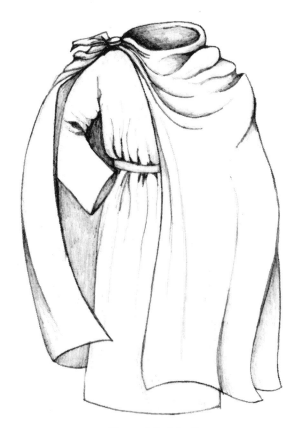

Figure 2.7 – Mantle

Headgear was an important component of the pre-Renaissance wardrobe. Heads were usually covered, even if only by a length of fabric tied around the head. To make the typical Arab-style headdress, cut a square of fabric about 20 inches square. Tie it down with a piece of cord or fabric. (See figure 2.8 on page 16.)

A monk's cowl plus a stocking cap is a typical Near Eastern style. To make a cowl: Cut a strip of fabric about 40" by 20". Sew into a tube. (For a small child, it should be about a third as big.) (See figure 2.9 on page 16.)

Figure 2.8 – Arab-style headdress

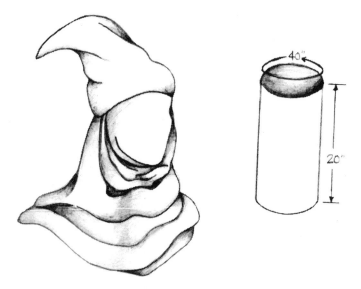

Figure 2.9 – Monk's cowl and stocking cap

Sloppy felt hats are appropriate for peasants through the Middle Ages and even into the Renaissance. You can make one by wetting a woman's felt hat and stretching it over a bowl. To widen the brim, cut a circle of felt and sew it on. (See figure 2.10 on page 17.)

The medieval warrior protected his head with a mail hood. Flexible armor (mail) can be simulated by the use of mesh-like materials that have a metalic thread woven into them. (See figure 2.11 on page 17.)

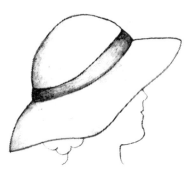

Figure 2.10 – Sloppy felt hat

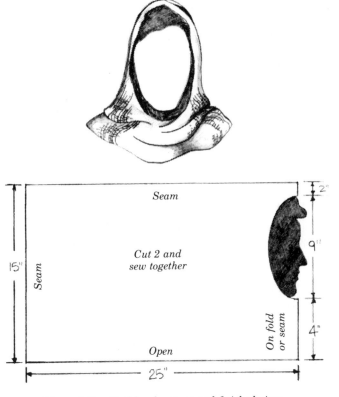

Seam

Cut 2 and
sew together

15"

Seam

Open

25"

On fold
or seam

2"

9"

4"

Figure 2.11 – Mail hood pattern and finished piece

Leg coverings and footwear: In ancient times, legs were apt to be bare. In colder climates, there were ill-fitting woolly stockings that went all the way up to the crotch (they looked like pants). Strangely enough, these stockings did not necessarily cover the foot. It is interestng to see that Greek soldiers might have leg guards, yet still have bare feet. Children's knitted stockings have been found dating from the fifth century. After that the art of knitting was apparently lost for about 10 centuries. Stockings were cut out of fabric, fitted and sewn, or made of leather. Grey-blue and dark grey were popular in medieval times, and patterned fabrics were also fashionable. Stockings were separate, not joined at the crotch. They did not always go beyond the ankle to cover the foot. Padding was used if it was seen as an improvement to the leg. Strips of material could be bound around the sole of the foot and up to the knees like puttees.

To make stockings, use either:

- narrow woolly pants
- long woolen underwear
- pajama pants
- leg warmers
- sweater sleeves
- tights

(See figure 2.12 on page 19.)

The amount of covering a leg needs depends also on the length of the tunic or robe. Often legs were bound, sometimes with stockings underneath.

In ancient times, the poor wrapped their feet in what they could find to protect themselves from the elements, or they went barefoot. In biblical times, sandals were appropriate for the Mediterranean area. By the Middle Ages, soft cloth or sometimes leather shoes were popular for those who could afford them, featuring pointed toes and laced ties on occasion. (See figure 2.13 on page 19.)

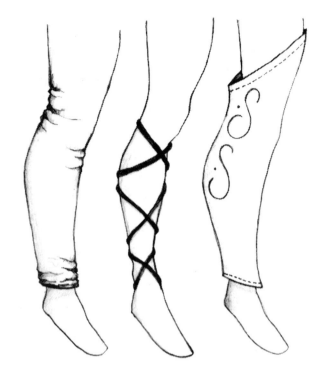

Figure 2.12 – Stockings

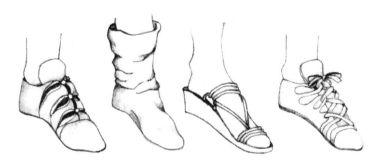

Figure 2.13 – Early times footgear

Renaissance

The Renaissance woman wore high-waisted, full-skirted, floor-length dresses, usually of heavy fabrics such as tapestry or velvet. Necklines were simple, but sleeves were fancy. She never went out without her head covered in some way, typically with a fabric matching her dress. (See figure 2.14.)

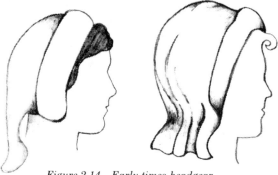

Figure 2.14 – Early times headgear

The 17th-century woman wore a shapeless dress of dark heavy fabric with a white collar or dickey over it. Typically, a part of the chemise (a shirt-like white undergarment) could be seen, as in the drawing from Brueghel's *Haymakers*. The chemise is showing at the sleeves and neck. You can get this effect by using a white blouse and putting a sleeveless, low-necked dress over it. (See figure 2.15 on page 21.)

Tucking up skirts was a practicality, to keep them cleaner. Sometimes the overskirt would be tucked up so that a coarse underskirt (like a petticoat) would be left to take the beating. Aprons, clogs or heavy shoes, and scarves complete the picture. Headscarves are also useful for covering modern, unpeasant-like hair.

For romantic, unrealistic peasant dress, you can find pictures of peasants in festival dress . . . what peasants wore on special occasions, and what I also think of as "musical comedy" style, although realism has invaded

Figure 2.15 – Clothing of a peasant. Apron or skirt is gathered up and tucked in to allow underskirt to show.

musicals too.

For men, the tunic grew into a large, long shirt by the 16th century. To make a long shirt, just add on similar fabric. Men's shirts were either gathered at the neck like a woman's peasant blouse (attractive on slender men only), or they had wide collars and full-cut sleeves with cuffs. (See figure 2.16 on page 22.)

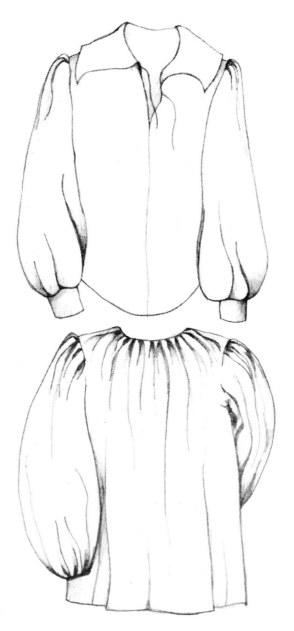

Figure 2.16 – Men's Renaissance shirts

To make the nongathered shirt, start with a regular man's shirt. Take off the buttons and the pocket, and sew up the front. Remove the collar — leaving the stand — and add softer collar like this: (See figure 2.17.)

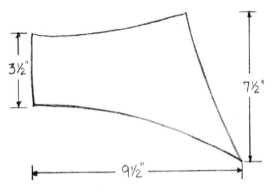

Figure 2.17 – Collar pattern

Remove the old sleeves, and add new, full ones, making sure you use a permanent press fabric since ironing full sleeves is a terrible job. Old no-iron sheets do very well. If you must make your gathered shirt from scratch, use a man's shirt pattern for the front and back, adding 6" to the width of both. Cut the front without the opening. Use a full sleeve from another pattern, or add 8" to 10" to the center of the regular sleeve for fullness. Use elastic or a drawstring instead of a cuff. (See figure 2.18 on page 24.)

A tabard is one of the fastest ways to costume Renaissance servants, heralds, and messengers. With it you can use a leotard (or some knitted top like a black turtleneck) and tights. (See figure 2.19 on page 24.)

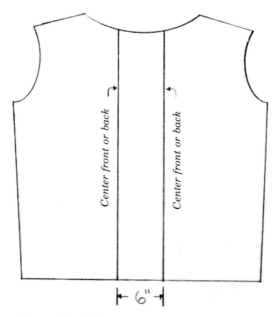

Figure 2.18 – Shirt pattern with addition of fullness

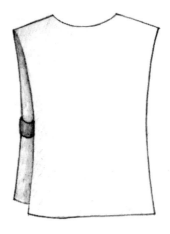

Figure 2.19 – Tabard

Different cultures sported wide varieties of headgear during the Renaissance era. The beret was often seen in the court as well as on gentleman callers or even travelers. Berets are fairly simple to make, as illustrated here: (See figure 2.20.)

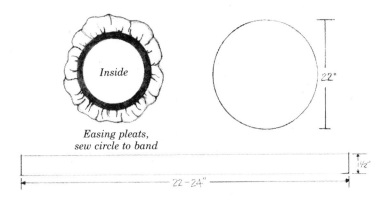

Easing pleats, sew circle to band

Figure 2.20 – Beret pattern

Gentlemen in the 1700s wore the tricorn reminiscent of the Three Musketeers as well. (See figure 2.21.)

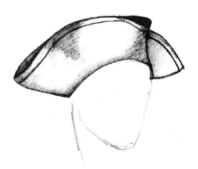

Figure 2.21 – Tricorn

25

You have to be pretty desperate to make a tricorn; not that it's so hard or time-consuming, but the nature of a tricorn is such that it's difficult to make it come out Brooks Brothers. Nevertheless, the effect is very possible. If you have a felt crown with a brim of some sort, you're ahead, since all you'll need to do is add more felt to make the brim wide enough to turn up. If you have to make your crown, stretch a wet piece of felt over a plastic styrene head — you'll be amazed at how much it will stretch. Tie it down with a piece of string and let it dry. This will result in a fairly shallow crown. Cut a brim about 4" wide (better use two thicknesses) and zigzag onto crown. To make it stiff, paint with clear varnish. Before the varnish dries, turn up brim and pin it to the crown the way you want it. Varnish takes a few days to get really dry and lose its odor. Sew trim on the outer edge.

Renaissance stockings were still sewn rather than knitted. Patterned fabrics were popular, and in Italy it was stylish to wear a stocking of a different color on each leg. In 1589, the first stocking frame was invented. As you might expect, silk was a luxury until the appearance of nylon.

Feet grew just a little fancier with the approach of the Renaissance, with the addition of heels, bows, and buckles to the basic shoe. The character who must appear bootless when a boot is the right footwear looks out of place. But for the costumer on a tight budget, paying even $10 for a used pair of boots may cut too deeply into the purse. There are alternatives.

To make a boot, cut a foot and leg pattern out of vinyl. Extend the boot top to the appropriate height. It's a good idea to make them high enough to use as an 18th-century boot also. You can always turn them down, either on the inside or the outside, if you want them shorter.

After you have made the foot and leg, take your construction to your friendliest shoe repairman. Ask him to sew this onto a sole (which he will supply). A couple of years ago, this entire job cost me five dollars — plus the complaining my shoe repairman did! Apparently vinyl is hard to work with. If by some miracle you could acquire a piece of leather, at least for the foot part, maybe it would be an easier job. It's also a good idea to save any extra vinyl, as you may want to make a cuff.

Trying to make a boot out of shoes using a vinyl leg is awkward, but not impossible. Cut a length of vinyl to cover the calf, with or without a cuff at the top. Add this above a pair of jodphur boots. At the joining point, make another cuff to cover the gap. You can use different colors of shoe polish to blend the leg with the boot. (See figure 2.22.)

Figure 2.22 – Boot

Colonial

Colonial times were, by necessity, simple times for the most part. Above all else, everyday clothing had to be functional. So unless you're costuming an elegant lady, whose dress would reflect the European style of the period, you can begin with a simple dress in an earth shade. A gathered skirt, as full as possible, was stylish and could be easily lengthened just by adding a length to the bottom to cover the ankles. To add to the sleeves and the skirt, use a compatible fabric, preferably one with a small print. With a bit of extra thought, you can achieve an integrated effect. Cover the seams with grosgrain ribbon or narrow bands of fabric (this can be a third fabric). You can cut off a few inches of the original fabric from the bottom of the skirt and the end of the sleeves and sew it on the bottom of the newly added pieces. More work, but probably more effective.

Add an apron made from a white pillowcase: Open up the pillowcase so that it's one big piece of fabric. If it needs to be shortened, keep in mind that the lower end is already hemmed and take the length off the top. Gather the top and attach a band (from an old sheet, maybe?) long enough to tie in a bow at the back. For an apron that goes all the way around, use two pillow cases. (See figure 2.23.)

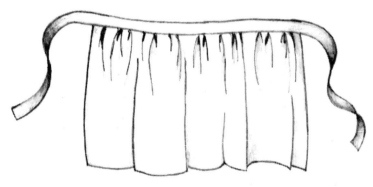

Figure 2.23 – Apron

Add a white collar and apron or a fichu or scarf, a square of white fabric about 22" by 22". Lop off a couple of inches for a small child. Decorate it with a row of lace. Fold to make a triangle. (See figure 2.24 on page 29.)

Figure 2.24 – Fichu or scarf

If your colonial lady has a special event to attend, or if she's wealthy, you might create a frock for her like the illustration on page 30. (See figure 2.25.)

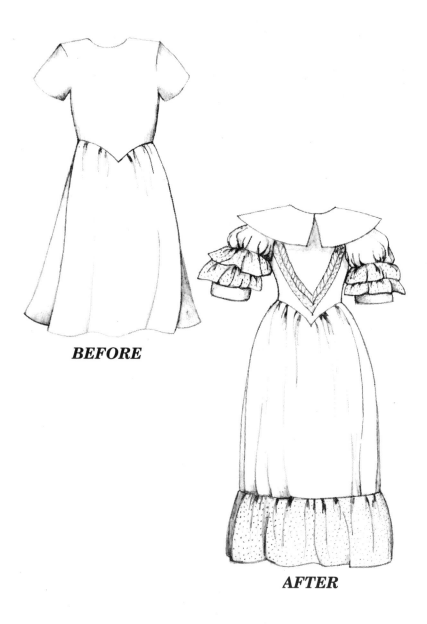

BEFORE

AFTER

Figure 2.25 – Add a white collar, some diagonal trim on bodice and add fabric to the bottom of the skirt and sleeves.

A painting called *Tailor's Workshop in Arles* by Raspail shows seamstresses in blouses, bodices, and skirts of different fabrics, obviously made of component parts: small-flowered print sleeves, plain bodices, striped skirts, large fichus. (See figure 2.26.)

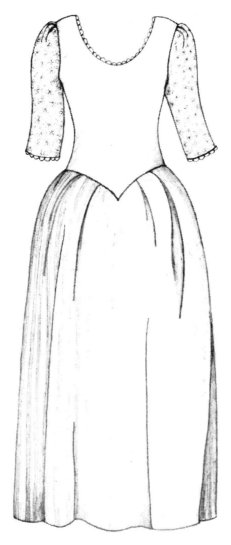

Figure 2.26 – Dress made from compatible scraps of fabrics

If you're working in the 18th century (and the Renaissance), keep a sharp eye out for compatible "scraps." A piece of fabric 15" by 30" can make a couple of sleeves. For a bodice you need something in the vicinity of 20" by 32". Learning to use scraps of fabric is as tricky as learning to use leftover food.

Colonial men frequently wore jackets, or doublets, with distinctive white collars. Make this jacket out of a plain jacket with no pockets and no lapels. Women's jackets can be used for boys. Pants-suit jackets are often a good beginning. For a small boy, a woman's vest will get you started. Just add sleeves and make it longer. It could also be sleeveless with another garment underneath. Collars were plain or lacy, but there were also coats with no collars. (See figure 2.27 on page 33.)

A full shirt made of Holland linen was usually worn under the jacket (doublet), but collars were attached on the outside.

Vests were very popular in the 18th century. If you're in a hurry — or short of fabric — you can make a vest with only a front. Fake the opening by sewing on buttons. (See figure 2.28 on page 34.) Sew ties on shoulders and at the waist. Ties go over the shoulders, and are tied to the ties at the waist. (See illustration.) A vest made this way won't hang as well as a vest that has a proper back, but it should do nicely for the chorus men.

Buff coats were not beautifully tailored. Make a reasonable facsimile from a tan sweatshirt. (See figure 2.29 on page 35.) Cut off hood, cuffs, and waistband. Remove zipper and front pockets. Add buttons and shape front into a point. Add trim at the waist for a more period look. A woman's straight-cut jacket will work, too. A long sweater is another possibility.

For an 18th-century shirt, either cut off the collar (not the stand) on a regular white shirt, or turn it to the inside (in case you want to use it again with the collar) and stitch it down. A jabot or stock will hide the shirt collar. If you use a stock (a long white neck scarf), a few

Figure 2.27 – Men's jackets (doublets) with optional waist seams

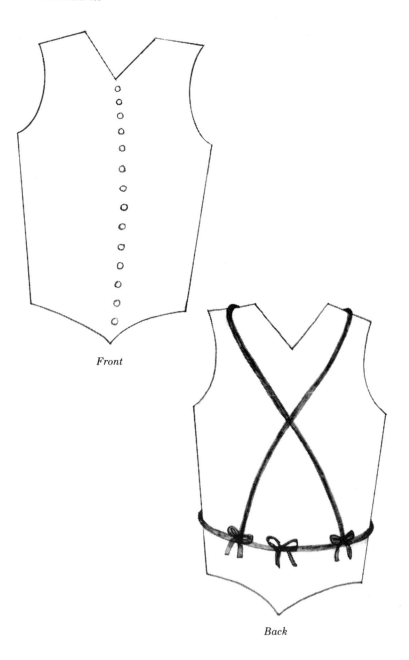

Front

Back

Figure 2.28 – Vest

A

B

C

D

Figure 2.29 – Tan sweatshirt transformed into several styles of buff coats. Example D shows a jabot collar.

inches of the shirt may show above the vest. With a jabot the shirt will be covered up. Nor will the cuffs show, since you will have had to add a lace ruffle onto them. You might wonder why have a shirt at all. The lace ruffle could be sewn to the inside of the coat sleeve, but remember that a shirt will protect your costume and the performer will likely feel better wearing a shirt. (Refer to figure 2.29 on page 35.)

The standing collar goes on through the 19th century. Turn up the collar on a regular shirt, modify the points so that they won't meet under the chin. Turn-down collars began in the second half of the century. Just make the points the shape you want. For a Lord Byron collar (wide Romantic) add a collar the shape of the one in figure 2.17 on page 23. If a coat is to be worn all the time, you won't have to bother adding full sleeves.

Calf-length, or just below the knee, pants went with the doublet. Cut-off elastic top women's pants work better for this effect, because they have less detail: no pockets, no fly. Colors should be earthy, since bright dyes were not readily available. To make knee breeches, cut off regular men's pants. If the pants are too wide at the knee, just take up the seams. For a more tailored look, you can leave a two-inch slit on the outside seam, or sew some buttons on the seam. The fly in the pants will not be historical, but if it's worn with a sash or a coat, it will hardly be noticeable. (See figure 2.30 on page 37.)

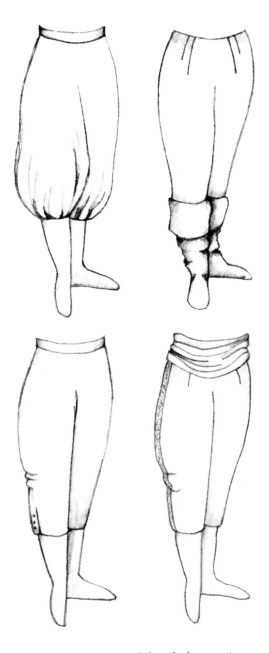

Figure 2.30 – Men's below-the-knee pants

With just a relatively minor operation, a large-size lady's coat becomes a man's coat representative of the late 18th or early 19th century as illustrated here. (See figure 2.31.)

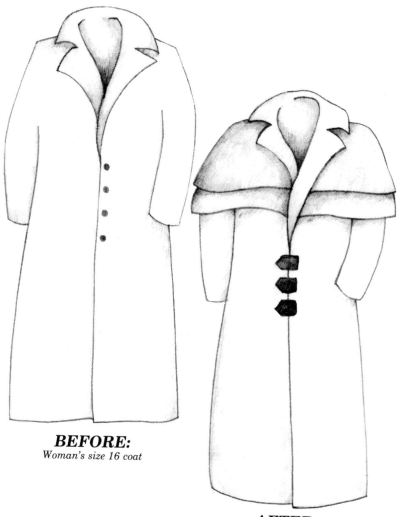

BEFORE:
Woman's size 16 coat

AFTER:
Men's coat of the late 18th, early 19th century with 2 capes and fastenings added.

Figure 2.31

Until the middle of the 18th century, children's clothes were carbon copies of their parents'. Just because you were a child did not mean you were any less corseted, that your hairdo was less fancy, or that your heels were less high.

After 1750, an effort was made to simplify children's clothes. Corsets became less armour-like, clothes were more loosely hung, and there were fewer of them. It was the ever practical, sporty English who first lifted these burdens. Children's styles, of course, have always followed those of adults, just as they do now; but whether they did so in general or in every last detail was the difference. It was not until the 20th century that clothes were made especially with children in mind.

Up to recent times, little boys (boys no more than six years old; in the 18th century and earlier, more like three or four) were dressed like girls, with dresses and curls.

Little girls often wore bonnets to protect themselves from the elements. The illustrations following show how simple it is to make a sunbonnet for a child.

- Cut rectangle 17" x 6".
- Make a channel in it for a gathering string.
- Cut a band 40" x 2".
- Cut a slightly circular piece 17" x 5".

(See figure 2.32 on page 40.)

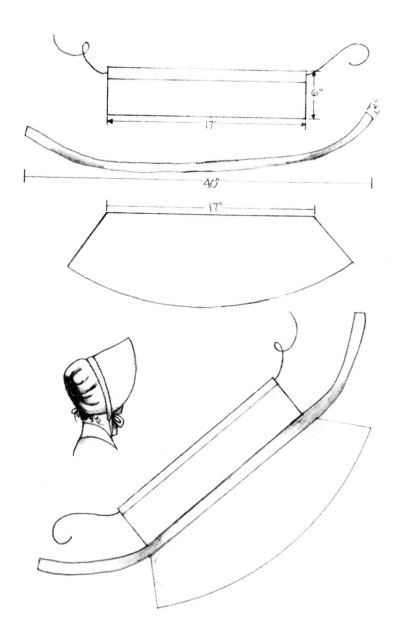

Figure 2.32 – Little girl's sunbonnet

The colonists and early settlers were frequently dismayed at the clothing (or lack of it!) worn by the Indians. To dress a small girl Indian style, start with a pillowcase. Cut neck and armholes, and cut fringe. (See figure 2.33.)

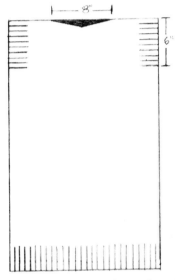

Figure 2.33 – Little girl's Indian-style tunic

You'll want to dye it, of course. For a bigger child or an adult, use a tunic pattern in an earthy shade. Cut fringe and use some of the easy new fabric paint to simulate ceremonial costume.

Buffalo shirts were originally made of hide. As you can see in the illustration, these were relatively shapeless. (See figure 2.34 on page 42.) A buff, tan, or brown sweatshirt with the cuffs and waistband removed can be used. Decorate with fringe and Indian designs: geometric patterns, drawings of buffaloes, bows and arrows, etc. (To lend an air of authenticity and avoid offending any native Americans

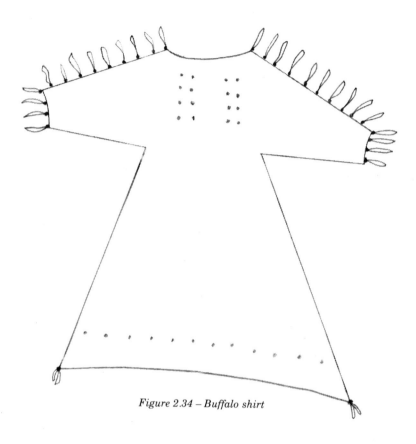

Figure 2.34 – Buffalo shirt

in your audience, do a little research at the local library before indiscriminately painting designs on your costumes.) Shirt length is below the knees. Leggings with trim cover legs, and feet can be bare or moccasin clad.

A breech cloth wraps around the crotch and comes up inside a belt, over it, and hangs down both in front and in back. The cloth is about 8" wide and 60" long, depending on how far you want it to hang down. Wear it with leggings or with pants that have the crotch cut out. The pants also hang from the belt. Tubes of cloth would work in place of pants. Use earthy shades, of course. A blanket can be worn over one shoulder and wrapped around the waist. (See figure 2.35.)

Figure 2.35 – Breech cloths

The earliest neckwear came along in the 17th century and was actually a white scarf (probably silk) about four feet long, called a cravat. Some were made of lace, some had lace trim on the ends. It covered the front of the shirt (occasionally a shirt ruffle might peek out.)

Typical for colonial men was the unplumed tricorn that reminds us of Paul Revere. The colonists also adapted it to the bicorn as illustrated here. (See figure 2.36.)

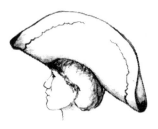

Figure 2.36 – Bicorn

Women kept their heads covered to be stylish, to be modest, and to protect themselves from the sun. Bonnets were definitely in for everyday wear, and large-brimmed hats with lots of ribbon and flowers were a luxury. (See figure 2.37 on page 45.)

The following illustrations should provide you with some idea of what colonial men and women wore on their feet. Men's shoes can easily be adapted by adding big buckles made of cardboard and painted to match the shoe. Either tie the buckle to the lacing or use a strap of elastic that goes underneath the sole of the shoe. (See figure 2.38 on page 45.)

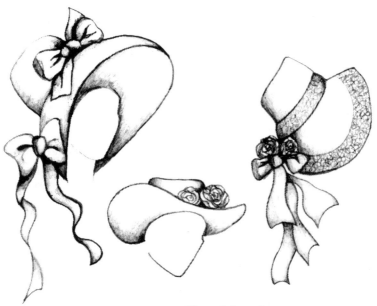

Figure 2.37 – Women's bonnets

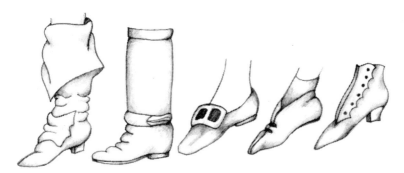

Figure 2.38 – Men's and women's Colonial period footgear

Boots were sloppy with bent-over tops, a look you can create by adding vinyl to regular boots. There is such a wide variety of styles on the market today for women that you might even find something in a store that would closely resemble the high-top, multibutton or lace-up styles that were popular for the ladies of the 1700s and

45

early 1800s. If your budget is already out of control and shoes are an item you'll be skimping on, try constructing a piece of felt to cover the ankle and slip over the top edge of your ladies' shoes. From a distance it might work.

1800 to World War I

Styles for women changed rapidly for a variety of reasons. The high-waisted empire style was popular early in the 1800s, featuring very light fabrics, semifull skirts, little sleeves, and low necklines. (See figure 2.39 on page 47.) You may find some old formal wear from the mid '50s or early '60s in the thrift shops that will adapt easily to this style.

In the 1830s, the natural waistline settled back in with medium-full skirts, medium-weight fabrics, and dropped shoulders. (See figure 2.40 on page 48.)

Then, in the 1840s, the pointed waistline appeared, and it could be seen well into the late '60s. Again we see medium weight fabrics and dropped shoulders, but skirts were getting fuller. The bell-shaped sleeve was popular. (See figure 2.41 on page 49.)

When we think of the period of the Civil War, we think of Scarlett O'Hara as the trendsetter. Keep the pointed or natural waist, but make the skirt very full and add lots of petticoats or a hoop. Plenty of ruffles and flounces will complete the outfit for your Southern belle. If you have a reasonably full skirt to start with, you can achieve an effect of greater fullness in the back to get a better period look. Add a new and full skirt a few inches down from the waist of the original skirt.

A fitted bodice may seem a paltry beginning, but these dresses are a long way from start to finish, and a perfectly fitting top is a good start. Mix and match those satins and taffetas from old formals which often compliment each other to create the Scarlett O'Hara look. (See figure 2.42 on page 50.)

BEFORE:
Lightweight cotton formal

AFTER:
Sleeves and trim added

Figure 2.39 – Empire style of the 1800s

47

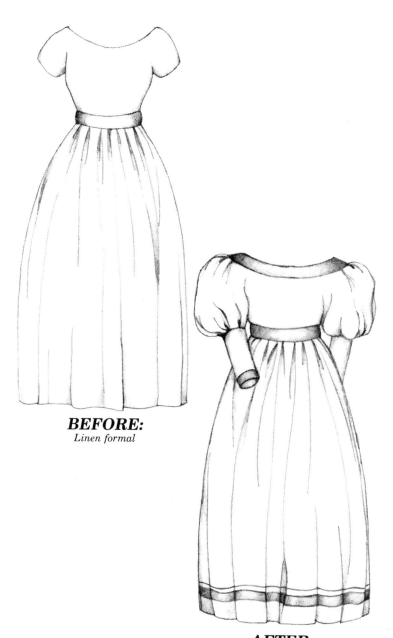

BEFORE:
Linen formal

AFTER:
Sleeves and trim added

Figure 2.40 – Romantic style of the 1830s

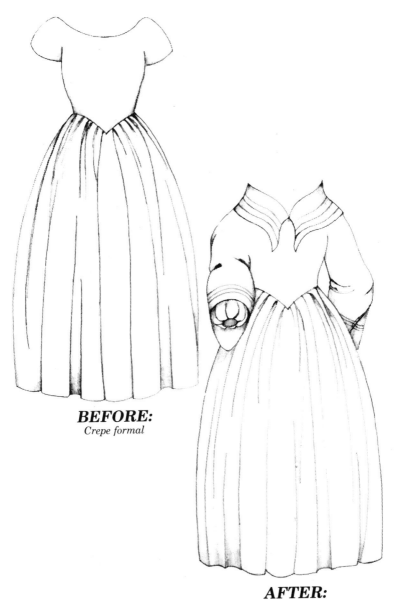

BEFORE:
Crepe formal

AFTER:
Bell sleeves with white cotton insert
added. Collar and trim added.
Petticoats worn to make skirt look fuller.

Figure 2.41 – 1840s pointed waistline

BEFORE:
Black velvet fitted top

AFTER:
*Add black taffeta skirt and ruffles. Red
satin quilted lining fabric used for
sleeves and streamers.*

Figure 2.42 – The Scarlett O'Hara look

Civil War dresses were wildly decorated and trimmed. (The sewing machine, patented in 1846 by Elias Howe, made dresses more complicated and life much simpler.)

The 1870s and '80s were a complex and cumbersome time with all the draping and the bustles that were so popular. The simplest way to create this look is to use a basic princess-style dress and pull the fullness to the back for a bustle effect. To do this, put the dress on your actress, then experiment by grasping the skirt at the seams in front or in back depending on the existing fullness, and then pull the material around to the back. Arrange in pleats or folds and sew down on either side of the placket, allowing pleats or folds to stand out to make a full effect. (See figures 2.43 and 2.44 on pages 52 and 53 respectively.)

When researching a costume, the first thing to consider is the waistline. Is it straight, natural, high, long, or pointed? In early times tunics and robes characteristically had straight waistlines. From then on seven basic variations evolved. They are:

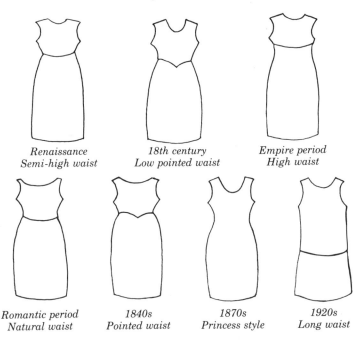

Renaissance	*18th century*	*Empire period*
Semi-high waist	*Low pointed waist*	*High waist*

Romantic period	*1840s*	*1870s*	*1920s*
Natural waist	*Pointed waist*	*Princess style*	*Long waist*

51

BEFORE:
Princess style silk dress

AFTER:
*Fullness at bottom of skirt is pulled up
and back for bustle effect. An added
underskirt will show beneath.*

Figure 2.43

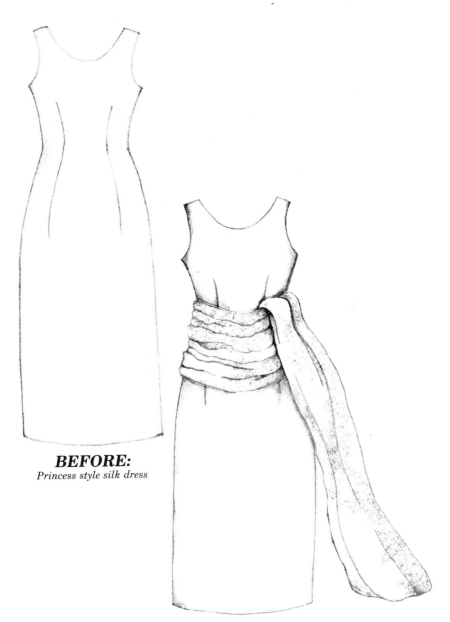

BEFORE:
Princess style silk dress

AFTER:
Flowered drape added

Figure 2.44

A bustle can be constructed of coat hangers as illustrated here. Just cover the frame with cotton or strips of fabric to keep the wires from showing through. Use more wire joints if the bustle doesn't seem secure. (See figure 2.45.)

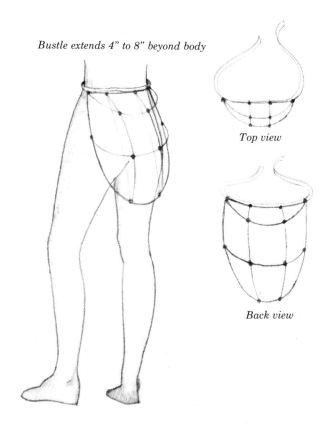

Bustle extends 4" to 8" beyond body

Top view

Back view

Figure 2.45 – Bustle constructed from wire and tape

The layered look was in for the 1870s and '80s and continued into the '90s as shown here. (See figure 2.46.)

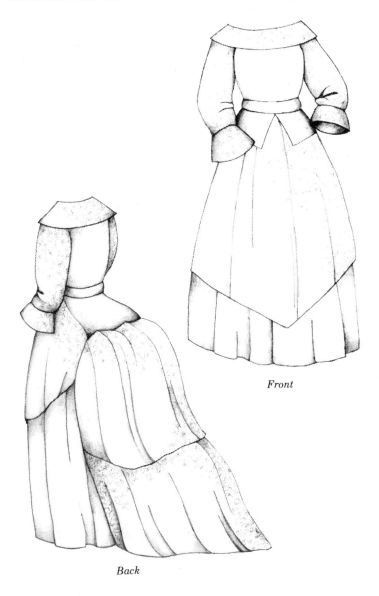

Front

Back

Figure 2.46 – Start with plain taffeta dress and add flowered drape and bustle. Add full sleeves and a dropped shoulder band.

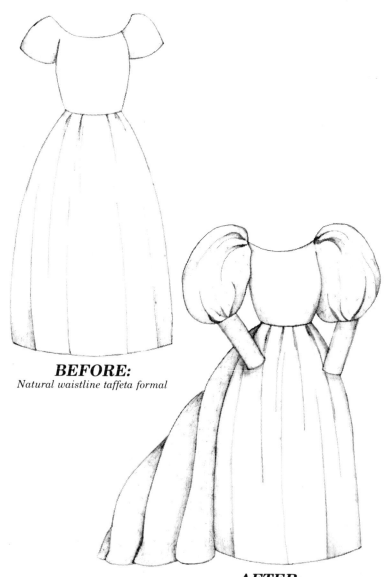

BEFORE:
Natural waistline taffeta formal

AFTER:
*Addition of leg-o-mutton sleeves, gored
skirt with train*

Figure 2.47

Figure 2.48 – Dress of pink silk (found with the front draping already done) was altered with cocoa brown puff sleeves and train

To drape, use a dress with a top that fits. Fake a peplum by sewing pieces of the dress (cut from the skirt or somewhere that won't show, such as sleeves or hem) onto a belt. Draping is basically a matter of a front and a back panel over a bustle. Put a wire bustle over the basic dress and then drape over it.

You may want to consult Janet Arnold's *Patterns of Fashion*. It's a big help to be able to see how different drapes were shaped. There are also some very good, fairly easy patterns in this book for turn-of-the-century skirts, which you probably would have to make since they are peculiar to that period.

With the new century, ladies' dresses became somewhat simpler. By 1910, the empire waistline had resurfaced, along with narrow skirts and underskirts. (See figure 2.49 on page 59.)

Until 1920, the waistline stayed fairly high. Dress shapes became quite singular: Gibson Girl, Peg-Top, Lamp Shade. The simplest was a tunic over a sheath as shown on page 60. (See figure 2.50.)

Female servants of this period can be appropriately dressed in high-necked, tight-sleeved, fairly full-skirted dresses of plain dark fabric. In general shape, dresses for servants followed current style. There were uniforms, of course, like the blue and white striped maid's dresses of the 1900s. Black dresses were popular from the turn of the century on. Aprons and caps were always distinctive and an important means of determining both period and status.

BEFORE:
Empire waist, narrow skirt, linen formal

AFTER:
Sash and trim added. Cut off lower skirt so the added underskirt with train is shown.

Figure 2.49

BEFORE:
Plain cotton sheath

AFTER:
*Put shorter flowered cotton sheath dress
over plain original*

Figure 2.50

MEN

Unless you're a fashion fiend, you'll agree that men's suits essentially swing back and forth between broad and slim lines. The silhouettes below show the extremes. (See figure 2.51.)

Figure 2.51 – Men's suits, slim and broad silhouettes

It was in the 1880s and '90s that suits began to appear. The Edwardian look (reappearing again in the 1960s) was close fitting, without cuffs, high-buttoned, with narrow lapels.

In the first decade of the 1900s the look began to broaden. Shoulders grew roomier and broader, lapels widened, cuffs appeared, and suits were sometimes double-breasted. In the second decade, the suit narrowed a bit in the shoulders and pants, and by 1920 the suit began working toward the wide look of the '30s and '40s. The crease in pants came in at the turn of the century.

Not many people will notice more than the general shape of a suit, so you should be able to find old suits that will adapt to the particular look you want. Older fabrics were heavier, louder, tweedier than fabrics were from the '40s on. To get a period look, concentrate on accessories such as ties, shirt collars, and hats.

Basically there are two kinds of collars: standing and turned down. However, it is the little variations in these that provide the important period clues. (See figure 2.52 on page 63.)

Tail coats are often needed for operatic choruses, weddings or symphony conductors. There is almost always a shortage, and a tail coat isn't something you can, or want to, just whip up. Sadly, those beautifully tailored relics worn by our great-grandfathers fit only the smallest of modern day men. A size 38 was enormous then; now, if you have an adult chorus, you may be lucky enough to use two of your heirlooms.

But there are ways of getting around the tail coat dilemma. One is to have a general or a colonel — military men in uniform. If you have any tail coats of colored fabric, decorate them as you would a uniform (epaulets, brass buttons, medals). Or if you can get any dress uniforms, use them. For the latter part of the 19th century, use military coats without tails. It's a good idea to avoid olive drab or khaki. Amazingly, a present-day coat decorated in a period way (stand-up collar, for instance) and mixed

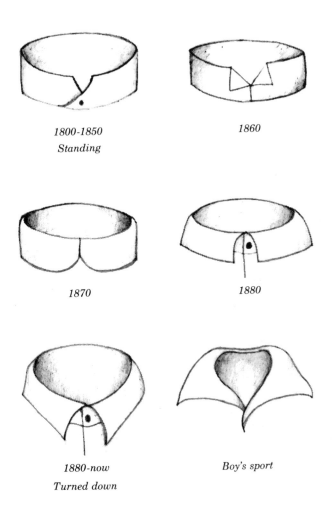

1800-1850
Standing

1860

1870

1880

1880-now
Turned down

Boy's sport

Figure 2.52 – Collars

with other period things, blends well.

For ethnic foreigners, have some men in robes or Nehru collars. These are hard to integrate in a serious production; better save them for a comedy, and even then it's nice to have some cooperation from your director so that these people can be given a few "reasons for being."

Once you have everyone in a coat and a pair of pants, you'll still have some alterations on the sleeves, waists, and pant lengths. Then you will need vests, and it's always surprising how differently vests fit. One thing you can do if you need a longer vest than you have is open up the shoulder seams and add a bit of fabric. If you're in a desperate hurry, take the back off completely, pin pieces of elastic from one shoulder to the other (around the back of the neck). Pin elastic at the waist and tie across the back. The point is that as long as you have a vest front, one way or another you can make it work. (Refer to figure 2.28 on page 34.)

After vests come formal shirts: ruffles from about 1800-1860 (just barely showing between cravat and vest), pleats until 1890 when starched bosoms came in. Fine, soft pleats came in again just before the '20s. The ruffles can be added to a regular white shirt. French cuffs help make a shirt more flexible. Don't fold them, and you'll get a few extra inches, or fold them not quite as high as they were meant to be. Sew on buttons, since the fewer cuffs links you have to cope with the better off you'll be, and it's very unlikely that any details such as these would be noticeable.

MINOR LEADS

Among the greater challenges to the costumer are the minor leads and the minor-minor leads. For example, in the first category of opera (Tosca) are characters like Angelotti. To begin with, who is he? A friend of the hero, and since the hero is a gentleman, one presumes Angelotti is too. But he has been in jail for a spell, so his gentleman's clothes should be tattered and torn, almost unrecognizable, as, indeed, the hero proclaims him to be. However, being a gentleman, he would have worn boots — an expensive proposition for someone who is only on stage for a few moments. Is there some way to avoid his having boots? Is it not possible that his boots might have been appropriated by his jailors? Or might they not have rotted away in the wet dungeon? And besides, wouldn't bare feet make him all the more poignant?

The minor-minor leads — servants, guards, laborers, innkeepers — are even worse because costume books contain so few pictures of the lower classes. Even the middle class is scarce, even after it comes into its own during the Industrial Revolution. Why costume books concentrate so heavily on the upper classes, I don't know. There are many paintings like Van Gogh's *Potato Eaters* that have never been reproduced. I have spent days peering into paintings hoping for a glimpse of the working classes, and a glimpse is usually about all I've managed; some vague figure in the background. I could hardly believe my eyes when I happened upon a painting featuring a Parisian street sweeper in 1818, (See figure 2.53 on page 66) and soon after in another book I found another showing a group of street workers in Paris in the mid-1800s. (See figure 2.54 on page 66.)

Figure 2.53 – Back view of a Parisian
street sweeper costume

Figure 2.54 – Street worker

Art department slide libraries are good places to look for paintings in which the working classes might be featured. Museums that keep tabs on our historical past may have photographs (the camera was invented in the mid-19th century). The hard facts are that the working classes were not popular as subject matter and that their clothes were worn out instead of saved.

Male servants in the 19th century in fashionable houses wore 18th-century styles — frock coats with lots of braid and knee breeches. In humbler households, male servants wore black tail coats in cheaper fabric, like the evening clothes of their masters. Toward the end of the century this became more popular universally. At the turn of the century, butlers began wearing black suits and black ties, but by the 1920s, white coats were in.

Bartenders and innkeepers in the 19th century wore long pants, vests, shirts with full sleeves, and a black tie that begins as a 5' by 2½" length of fabric that grew narrower midcentury to become a black string tie. A large apron is often an effective addition.

To create an overcoat for the well-dressed 19th-century gentlman, start with a lightweight man's coat. Widen the collar with a darker overlay and add matching cuffs. Fit the waist by cutting the coat off from the waist down. Put in darts above the waist and in the piece you have cut off, sew it back on. (See figure 2.55 on page 68.)

BEFORE:
Man's lightweight coat

AFTER:
Add wider dark collar and cuffs and take in waist

Figure 2.55 – 19th century men's overcoat

By the turn of the century, men's overcoats had become pretty impressive. To achieve the look, start with a greatcoat from the 1940s. Trim it with a fake fur collar and a matching band at the bottom as illustrated. (See figure 2.56.)

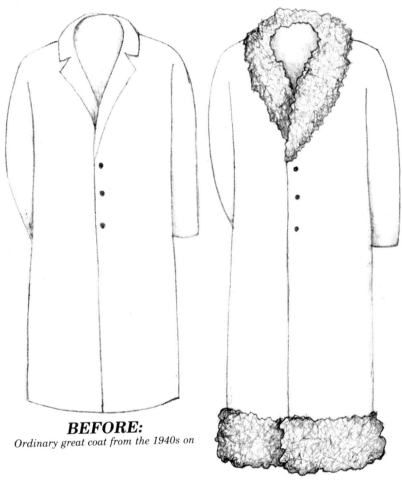

BEFORE:
Ordinary great coat from the 1940s on

AFTER:
Fake fur trim at collar and band at bottom added

Figure 2.56 – Turn-of-the-century man's coat

BOYS

In the early 1800s, big boys wore trousers like their fathers' and short jackets. By mid-century the jackets got a little longer. Big boys wore long pants until after the Civil War.

The sailor suit became popular in the 1870s (though it had been in existence for a century) and remained so in one version (with long pants or short) or another until well into the 20th century. Knickers appeared in the '70s. Knee pants (below the knee) became prevalent in the 1880s and stayed around until the 1930s. Lord Fauntleroy costumes — black velvet suit with a white lace collar and red sash — came along in the '80s. Fauntleroys were worn by boys ages eight to 10 or so. (See figure 2.57.)

Figure 2.57 – Lord Fauntleroy suit for boys

From the turn of the century into the 1920s and '30s, small boys wore sailor collars with short pants. Boys a little older wore shorts or knickers unless they were very dressed up, in which case they wore long pants. Eton collars and Windsor ties with blouses were quite popular, and caps were in vogue. (See figure 2.58.)

Figure 2.58 – Eton collar and Windsor tie

Big boys wore jackets without lapels, so that their blouse collars could be on the outside. Women's jackets and blouses work very well for boys. Add a wide white collar or a sailor collar and a tie for the proper look. Sailor suits (with long, wide-legged pants) were still in, as were Fauntleroy suits. Wool stockings were worn with laced oxfords (often high topped). Ankle-high tennis shoes appeared at this time as well.

GIRLS

Girls' dresses followed adult styles more closely than boys', the main difference being that their dresses were a little shorter. In the early 1800s, dresses were calf-length, worn with tubular ankle-length pantaloons. To make children's pantaloons, cut two pieces of fabric wide enough to go around the upper part of the leg (with a couple of inches to spare), and long enough to reach from the bottom of a panty leg to the ankle. Sew into tubes, sew onto panties, and decorate with lace.

By the 1840s, girls' hemlines crept up to midcalf, and that's where they remained until the 1930s. Stockings replaced pantaloons after the Civil War.

From the 1870s until after the turn of the century, long-waisted dresses and sailor blouses were popular for all young girls. Pinafores were also popular throughout the last three-quarters of the century. (See figure 2.59.)

Figure 2.59 – Girl's pinafores

Girls' sailor suits, kilted skirts, and middy blouses began to appear in the early 1900s. A ruffle, new sleeves or a sash, or a pinafore added to a child's own dress is a quick fix for costuming little girls. If the child hasn't a dress to spare, don't forget about the thrift shops.

For children who are supposed to look as though they lived on the street, you can use a wide range of garments as long as you keep within the general "shape" of the period. For instance, you wouldn't want to have children wearing narrow skirts when full ones were the only fashion. If the dress top isn't right, cover it with a jacket or sweater. You can also dress street children (like those in *Oliver* in the 1830s) in clothes that are too big or too small, since they would be wearing whatever they could get their hands on. Hats are great for transforming kids, and hats that are too big or too small can add a humorous or poignant touch.

Many cultures throughout the ages have considered it immodest for women to appear in public bareheaded. Puritan New England shared that view, and some remnant of it remained into the 19th century. But by the time of the Civil War, modesty became less an issue than practicality (hats for protection from the elements) and style (either big or small, but always feathered or flowered). (See figure 2.60.)

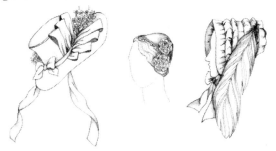

Figure 2.60 – Women's hats

Hats were in for both men and women at the turn of the century. For the gentlemen, Homburgs, fedoras, bowlers, and short top hats were popular, and the knitted watch cap was a frequent choice of the working class. These styles remained into the '30s. (See figure 2.61.)

Figure 2.61 – Men's hats

Headgear is definitely the final touch, and not as difficult to make as you might think. (See figure 2.62 on page 74.)

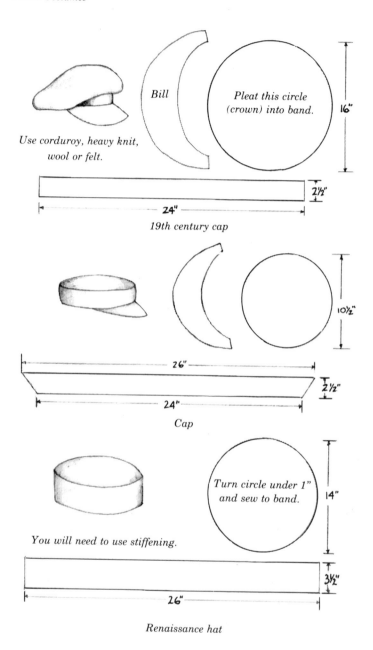

Bill

Pleat this circle
(crown) into band.

16"

Use corduroy, heavy knit,
wool or felt.

2½"

24"

19th century cap

10½"

26"

24"

2½"

Cap

Turn circle under 1"
and sew to band.

14"

You will need to use stiffening.

3½"

26"

Renaissance hat

Figure 2.62 – Patterns for men's caps

Don't overlook what can be done with just a plain few-inches-wide piece of material. A "rag" can be tied around a head and knotted in the back to identify an Arab, pirate, peasant, or gypsy.

To protect the feet and legs, leggings have been "in" since ancient times when they were called "leg guards." The American Indians wore leggings made of leather. Sometimes leggings went above the knee, but more often they stopped under the knee. They can be made of almost anything: leg warmers, burlap (tied over the calf), vinyl, canvas, or leather. Leg coverings for women are something of a puzzle, because dresses in drawings and paintings are carefully made to cover women's legs. Peasant women probably wore leggings under their skirts when it was cold. Probably, women who could afford them wore woolen stockings like those of the men. In the 1800s, women wore calf-length pantaloons. Silk stockings appeared around 1900, nylons not until the '40s.

The Industrial Revolution allowed shoe styles to come into their own as production moved from the cobbler's bench to the assembly line. (See figure 2.63.)

Figure 2.63 – Footgear

The Roaring '20s and the Depression '30s

You may be able to find authentic clothing, particularly if you're doing a school or church play. Encourage everyone to rummage through their attics. Thrift shops have small collections of early 20th-century clothing. The long-waisted style of the '20s may be the hardest to find, depending on the current design cycle. The chiffons of the '20s were distinctive. If you use the right kind of fabric, you can probably get the effect by using any straight vertical pattern, with the addition of a low-slung belt and maybe a big flower strategically positioned. Be careful mixing authentic costumes with newly-created ones; the authentic ones will spoil the effect of the new ones.

Dresses for the '30s and '40s are easier to effect because the natural waistline had returned. Crepe and chiffon were still distinctive fabrics, but certainly not all dresses were made of these two materials. You should be able to get the effect with some of the calf-length dresses from the late '40s and early '50s. Of course, genuine '30s and '40s dresses are also still around. (See figure 2.64 on page 77.)

BEFORE:
Evening suit from the mid-1970s

AFTER:
Draped neck piece added. Skirt made slimmer.

Figure 2.64 – 1930s or '40s formal

Ladies' hats were close fitting and simply decorated in this era. (See figure 2.65.)

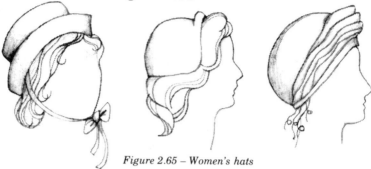

Figure 2.65 – Women's hats

Ladies' shoes ascended to new heights in the '20s and '30s, with the appearance of the stiletto heels we've since grown accustomed to. Pumps and straps were popular, and T-straps were especially popular for little girls.

The Fabulous Fifties!

Poodle skirts, petticoats, saddle shoes, white bobby sox, and ponytails were the only way for a teenage girl to look when she wasn't wearing pedal-pushers (knee-length pants) and one of her father's shirts with the sleeves rolled up. Her boyfriend wouldn't be seen without his T-shirt and jeans (comb in back pocket for keeping the hair slicked back, of course). Tough guys wore leather "motorcycle" jackets. The little woman dutifully stayed home with an apron around her trim shirtwaist (sans petticoats) and flat-heeled pumps. Her hair would be bobbed and comfortably curled. Dad wore his suit to work, and relaxed in his slacks and plaid shirt in the evening. "It was the best of times; it was the worst of times!"

To make the ever-popular circular skirt, fold a piece of material into quarters. (See figure 2.66 on page 79.) The width depends on how long the skirt has to be. Felt was a popular material, and appliques were in (such as a poodle). Cut two circles and sew them together. The waist will have lots of gathers and the skirt will be very swingy.

Figure 2.66 – The circular skirt with poodle applique

Chapter 3
WHO WAS THAT MASKED MAN?

Angels

A costume will turn any little imp into an angel! Start with the peasant blouse pattern we saw in Chapter 2, the one with a gathered neckline and full sleeves. (See figure 2.16 on page 22.) When you're cutting it, add the length you need to make it reach the ankles. If you want it very full, add fullness at the center, both back and front. Cut the sleeves wrist-length but don't gather them. (See figure 3.67 on page 82.)

Wings for angels — or butterflies, bees, bats, or other creatures — can be made by fusing layers of iron-on interfacing. Shirt bond is probably the heaviest. Hobby shops also have Pelon under Transfer Web. Use as many layers as you need for the stiffness you want. To add stiffness, bond this to stiff fabric, glue it to cardboard, or paint it. For variety or distinction, bond on decorations with Transfer Web, glue on pieces of paper or fabric, or paint designs. Before the layers get too thick, sew fabric straps to the middle to tie around the chest and come over the shoulders to anchor the wings. Wear a leotard and tights in the appropriate color. Match straps to leotard. Pin or sew to leotard to prevent slipping. (See figure 3.68 on page 83.)

Figure 3.67 – Angel robe

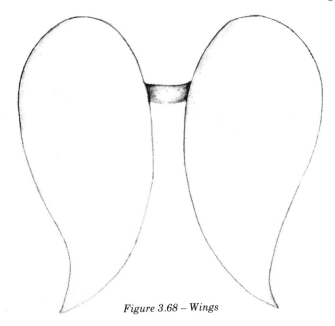

Figure 3.68 – Wings

Armor and Military

Flexible armor (mail) can be simulated by the use of mesh-like materials that have a metallic thread woven in. See the illustration in Chapter 2. (See figure 2.11 on page 17.)

If you can find the kind of vinyl used for automobile seats, it makes excellent armor. Some vinyl will take a long time to dry if you spray it with paint, so spray a week ahead of time. If sewing vinyl is difficult for your machine, try sewing on the wrong side. Cut armor from a vest pattern, without a front opening. Leave one or both sides open. Close with hooks and eyes or a period fastening of straps and buckles. Add a peplum. You'll probably have to cut the neck down and make the armholes larger. Armor can also be made of felt, or some other heavy materials; quilted fabrics are good. (See figure 3.69 on page 84.)

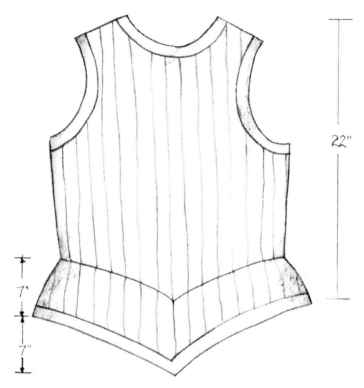

Figure 3.69 – Armor is trimmed with strips of vinyl that have been sprayed with silver paint and stapled on.

Military headgear very often suggests a specific time period; however, certain helmets were almost prototypes for all armies in the 19th century. (See figures 3.70 and 3.71 on pages 85 and 86 respectively.)

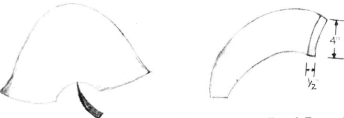

Helmet liner (modern)

Wood or heavy cardboard. To attach, drill 2 holes in helmet liner and screw into place.

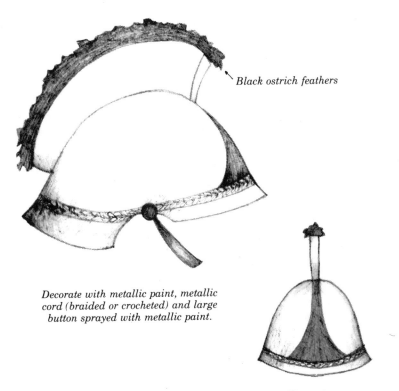

Black ostrich feathers

Decorate with metallic paint, metallic cord (braided or crocheted) and large button sprayed with metallic paint.

Front view

Figure 3.70 – Basic 19th century helmet, Napoleonic Wars. Look in Military Uniforms in Color *by Kannik for ways to decorate a basic helmet.*

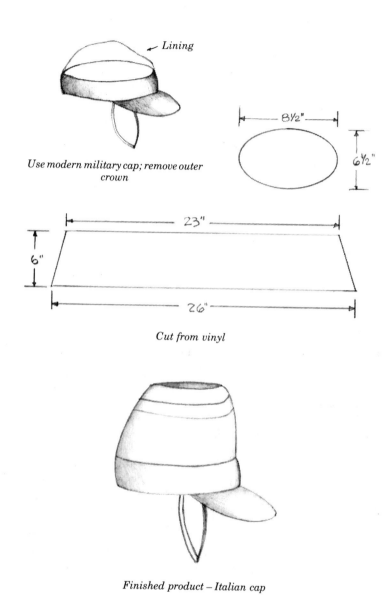

Lining

Use modern military cap; remove outer crown

8½"

6½"

23"

6"

26"

Cut from vinyl

Finished product – Italian cap

Figure 3.71 – Basic 19th century military cap or Shako. Check Kannik for variations on this theme. Cap could be straight (Mexican, Swiss) or wider at top (Russian, Brazilian).

Leggings are a poor man's godsend when it comes to costuming the troops. Like you, the troops were too poor to have boots. Over regular black shoes, cut leggings out of vinyl. For a pattern, use a pair of army surplus leggings. If you can't get any, approximate these shapes. (See figure 3.72.)

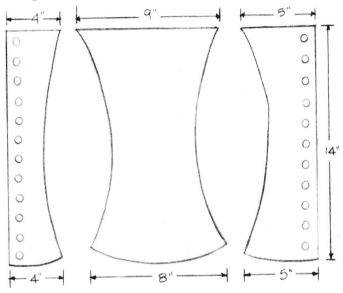

Figure 3.72 – Leggings or puttees pattern

Comedy

One way to express comedy is to introduce something inappropriate: a very tight, too small dress when the current style is loose fitting, for instance. Or clothes that are too young or too old for the age of the wearer, or a man wearing a diaper and a cut-off T-shirt with boots and a helmet or a baby bonnet. (Idea courtesy of Linda Dyer.) An overcoat with shoes, socks, and a hat, but no pants (what is worn under the coat is not our business) is my husband's idea of your friendly neighborhood flasher. Clothes that are too big, that don't go together — you can find all sorts of horrors at a thrift shop, like a wonderful drapey old lady's dress for a young girl.

Figure 3.73 – Monsters created with hosiery and stuffing

Monsters

(See figure 3.73 on page 88.) Lumpy, bumpy, misshapen creatures are easily created by stuffing a leotard or other close-fitting but stretchable garment with rags, towels, sheeting, or whatever's handy. Leotards and tights can be pretty expensive, especially if you must create a crowd of monsters. I've accomplished the same effect substituting several pairs of pantyhose and a turtleneck. Even when "runs" have made them useless for dress wear, pantyhose are quite acceptable for holding padding in place. Taking a page out of the criminals' handbook, a stocking over the head makes anyone's face a fright! Or stitch some feathers in strategic places and you're a bird.

South of the Border

For a festive fiesta look, think color! Start with a gathered skirt (the fuller the better) that fits. Decorate it with bands of fabric. Use both solid and compatible patterned fabrics. Ribbons make a colorful addition and save time, but if they aren't in the budget, use narrow bands of fabric.

There are patterns for peasant blouses, although you can probably find one already made. Adding full sleeves to a plain blouse will also do the trick. A bright scarf can be tied around the head, neck, or waist. (See figure 3.74 on page 90.)

Figure 3.74 – The fiesta look

A more exotic fiesta costume could look like this: (See figure 3.75.)

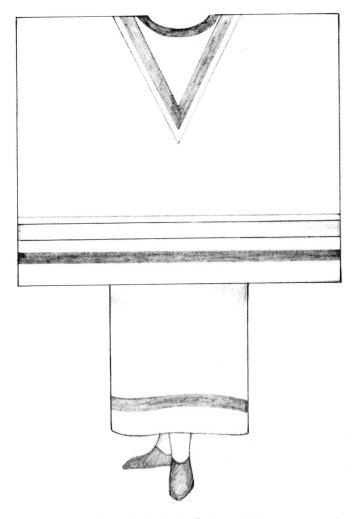

Figure 3.75 – Exotic fiesta costume

The undergarment could be a tunic or a straight skirt. The upper piece is as wide as the distance across the body from wrist to wrist, and hangs down to the knees. If your fabric is plain, decorate it with ribbons and bands of contrasting fabric or some inexpensive fabric paint available at most discount stores. Colorful flowers and braids with ribbons braided in make suitable hair dressing.

The pajama pattern makes an excellent outfit for a peon or field hand. White or nearly white fabric is most common in warm climates, but you may want to add a scarf for color. A Nehru collar and drawstrings at the ankles and wrists are typical but a cuff will make the outfit more elegant. A deeply frayed leg opening makes a different statement. And the men may want to try leaving a shirt unbuttoned and tying it at the waist. Spray-paint an ordinary farmer's straw hat with white — not all Latins wear sombreros. (See figure 3.76 on page 93.)

Figure 3.76 – Use a pajama pattern for a peon or field hand.

Wire Construction

When a tree must walk across a stage, it must have someone inside it or behind it. If your task is to create a moveable, wearable tree or some other large costume to represent an inanimate object, you must learn about wire construction. Stage supply stores sell wire designed for this purpose, but at a cost that may be out of reach for your limited budget. Don't despair! Coat hangers abound in most everyone's closets, and they're malleable yet sturdy. Baling wire or fence wire is also fairly inexpensive. With a pair of pliers, you can make a frame out of coat hangers. Stabilize it by sewing fabric over it. Don't worry about what color or pattern your fabric is, since the only way to produce those final realistic touches is by painting the fabric anyway. Wire construction requires some real planning and a lot of trial and error. It isn't my favorite task as a costumer, and after agonizing over a clock and a tree for a couple of Ravel operas, I thought I'd get to deposit the experience deep in my memory bank and move on. Not long afterwards, I was asked to make a tooth big enough to wear! A costumer's life is one of constant challenge, but then that's the joy of it.

Chapter 4
UNDERNEATH IT ALL

You get a note from Ms. Simmons: Your daughter will be playing Cinderella in the class play. Can you provide the costume? Including the undergarments? If you search the books at the library for information on proper underwear for would-be princesses long, long ago in a far-away land, you're likely to go home empty handed. Here are some interesting bits and pieces I've collected over the years.

Undergarments

A *chemise,* or shift, is a blouse-length white garment made of washable material. (See figure 4.77.) Affluent

Figure 4.77 – Chemise or shift

women in the Middle Ages wore them under their dresses. If you look at paintings from these times to the 19th century, you can see the white outline of this undergarment, more often at the sleeves but sometimes as a yoke. Sometimes it's just a ruffle showing at the neck. In the 18th century, the sleeves became short and the neck was cut low. In the 19th century, the chemise was less likely to show on the outside. The modern slip evolved from the chemise late in the 1920s, which is when underwear as we know it was born.

Drawers (knee length) first appeared in Italy in the 16th century, and may have been worn in Germany and Holland. (See figure 4.78.) But they weren't universally

Figure 4.78 – Knee-length drawers with drawstring waist

accepted until well into the 19th century. In the 1850s, when skirts began to widen, calf-length pantaloons appeared and were worn along with a chemise, corset, and many petticoats.

To make *pantaloons,* cut two tubes big enough to go

around the legs, sew to underpants, and decorate with lace. (See figure 4.79.)

Figure 4.79 – Pantaloons

The number of *petticoats* increased as the skirts grew fuller. As you shop the thrift shops and garage sales, keep an eye open for that senior prom formal from the '40s or '50s. Made almost entirely of net, these dresses make excellent petticoats; much better than crinoline which costs more and must be starched and ironed when washed. Net dresses are light enough not to cost much when you clean them at the self-service cleaners, and they don't lose their stiffness. Just cut off the skirt of an old net formal, all layers at once. Sew an elastic band on at the waist. The coarser the net, the stiffer the petticoat, of course.

It's my opinion that nothing can do more for a not-quite-expensive-enough, not-quite-heavy-enough dress than a good petticoat underneath it. A trademark of a less-than-professional production is inadequate underpinnings. Petticoats really are very important, both to give weight to a period dress, and to help it hang attractively. A full skirt in motion swings back and forth, and too much leg may be seen when a petticoat isn't worn, ruining the period effect.

As for hoops, bustles, and all the paraphernalia that makes skirts stick out in certain places, in many cases just going for effect is better than the real thing — more graceful and easier to handle when the wearer isn't super experienced. Very wide hoops and enormous bustles are apt to look silly, and a great many thicknesses of fabric are required to cover the substructure. Underneath Civil War styles there were usually about six petticoats. You'll get a horrible surprise if you put a big wide hoop under one layer of material. A modest hoop will give the effect you want, besides being easier to work with. It's a good idea to let anyone wearing a hoop practice with it to see how much space it takes and how it feels.

When the hoop went out and skirts no longer swung about, pantaloons became pantalettes — two separate tubes attached to a band. Toward the end of the century, the tubes were joined and cut fuller. Just when they became knee-length or joined, no one seems to know exactly. By the 1920s, drawers shortened into loose-legged panties, and from then on grew scantier.

Corsets of one kind or another were worn from the beginning of time until after World War I. (See figure 4.80 on page 99.) From skin to outer layer, the order was: chemise, stockings, drawers, corset, corset cover or camisole (a fancy corset cover), and petticoats.

Many performers don't seem to be aware that the no-bra look is an absolute flop when it comes to period clothes. A mistake I've made too many times is fitting a costume without pinning the performer down about underwear. Especially when there are more than a few extra pounds. It's amazing how those pounds can be shifted around by various kinds of undergarments. It also took me a while to recover from the first college student I had in a chorus who couldn't produce a single pair of ordinary stockings.

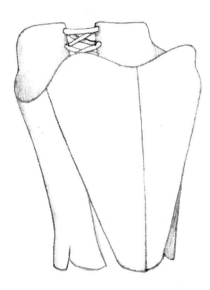

Figure 4.80 – Corset

Nightshirts first appeared in the Middle Ages. Before that, people either slept in the nude or in their day clothes. In the 19th century, night clothes became a part of everyone's wardrobe. Men wore nightshirts until about 1900, when pajamas came into vogue. Women's nightgowns were high-necked, straight, full, white, washable garments. The amount of pleating and lace, not the style, represented the main difference between rich and poor until the 1920s. Crocheted trim was popular on chemises, drawers, and nightgowns. In the '20s, bodices on nightgowns were crocheted. Trim was essential to the stylish underwear wardrobe.

Chapter 5
HELPFUL HINTS AND USEFUL INFORMATION

Hems and Zippers

We've all seen the picture: The man smokes his cigar, fidgets, and fumes while his wife hems *her* dress as *he* wears it. Actually, I seem to have just as much success hemming a dress that's on a hanger as one that's on a person. I discovered this after a Southern belle stood patiently while I carefully measured the six-foot-long hem of her frock every few inches from the floor. Afterward, when I hung the dress on a hanger, it still didn't look right, and I felt obliged to work on it some more. When she tried it on again, it was even.

So my advice is this: Don't waste anyone's time or try their patience. Pin hems while the garment hangs on a hanger. Just even up the shoulder seams and measure from the waist every few inches. This will be every few feet at the bottom if the skirt is full. If you have no waist seam, measure from under the arms. If you pin your hem so that it looks right as it hangs, chances are you'll be very close to an even hemline.

Never underestimate the importance of proper hemming. Hemlines can be seen from every seat in the theater, and an uneven one is very distracting. The musical and dramatic aspects can seem so much more important, especially when they are very good. But this is particularly so when all other aspects are excellent. You should take care, because you don't want to distract from a good performance, which is what happens when little details — like hemlines — are not right. Remember that spray starch can be your savior when it comes to eradicating old hemlines.

Knowing what the audience will be able to see can

be bewildering, especially to a beginner. When you must budget the time you spend in finishing a garment, let the distance between the apron and the first row be the criterion. If the audience is right up under the stage, your sewing will have to be more finished looking than it would be in a bigger theater. Hand hemming may be in order. (Slight stains or fading — not uncommon in bargain materials — will show also.) But if you have about twenty feet between the apron and the first row, you can commit all sorts of crimes. Probably, if there is this much space, the theater will hold as many as 600 to several thousand seats. A machine hem could be seen from about the first dozen rows, but it will probably go unnoticed. The rest of the theater can't see it at all. Nor will they notice if you use white thread on light fabrics and black on dark. Thread has become expensive enough to economize in this way. By watching for sales and worrying less about matching colors exactly, you'll save dollars, not just cents. My personal philosophy is that every aspect of a production deserves the careful attention of one person. When costumes are my responsibility, I want to give them the best I have to offer within the budget or time constraints that may exist.

You can also save money on zippers if you buy at Goodwill or the Salvation Army where second-hand zippers are as little as 25 cents. (Multiply the savings if you've got to buy 15 zippers and the fabric store wants $1.95 each!) If you're using zippers that don't exactly match your fabric, cover up the zipper as much as possible or dye the zipper before you install it. If it matches, you may sew it in quickly, disregarding puckers and other faults.

I don't recommend spending the time to sew up the seam before you put the zipper in and then rip it out once the zipper's in place. With a little practice, you should be able to do a good enough job by just pinning the zipper in and sewing. Unique zippers, much as I like them for regular sewing, are harder to unzip and can cause problems if there isn't a dresser or a lot of time for getting into and out of a costume. Invisible zippers never seem to work for me at all. Side zippers are harder to put in, more apt to make a bulge. Use back openings whenever you can. Some people worry about zippers not being invented before the '30s. This, again, I think is a kind of authenticity better left to the motion picture industry, especially if there is no use of the zipper on stage.

Sewing in Sleeves

Bodices or vests may be reused time and time again by adding different sleeves. I have devised a system that allows me to sew a new sleeve in very quickly: Match shoulder seam dot to shoulder seam. Match underarm seam to side seam. Pin in both places. Pull, easing thread up so that sleeve fits armhole. Start sewing on the machine on either side of the fullness. That way, if there is any extra fullness or if the sleeve has been pulled up too tightly, you can make an adjustment just before you finish sewing. Elaborate basting, with either pins or thread, is not necessary in costume sewing. (See figure 5.81.)

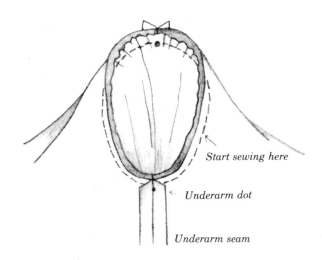

Start sewing here

Underarm dot

Underarm seam

Figure 5.81 – Set-in sleeve

There may be a time when you need to make an armhole that allows lots of freedom for the arms, while it may also be important not to have the costume moving up and down at the same time (for instance, when someone is dancing). One way is to slit the costume under the arm and wear some sort of matching stretch undergarment. Another way is a small, tight-fitting armhole. For this you must have a good tailor and several fittings. Still another way is to put in a gusset. If you don't mind the extra bulge (in a robe it will never be noticed) when the arms are down, this is the easiest thing to do.

It seems appropriate to mention here that you can fake a dropped shoulder by covering the existing sleeve seam with some sort of decorative collar or band. The result will have the desired effect and be more comfortable at the same time. (See figure 5.82.)

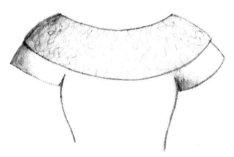

Figure 5.82 – Dropped shoulder neckline

Too Much of a Good Thing: Leftover Fabric

Everyone who sews has faced the same dilemma: Which scraps do you keep and which ones do you throw away? When I first started working for the Colorado Springs Opera Association, I inherited what was referred to as the Guts Box. Every single little piece of fabric that had been cut off anything for years was waiting there for me, including several nice dirty old lengths of hem that were indeed like entrails.

However, every now and then, the saving of a piece

of fabric you're sure was not worth a dime ends up saving you hours. Costumers with low budgets often get desperate. Nevertheless, always think through the possibilities. Is the costume you made the sort that you might want to enlarge someday? A little leftover scrap might just do the trick. Or, would the scraps be good for trim? Or is there enough leftover fabric for a transformation? Along with the Guts Box, I inherited a man's corduroy suit with a waist-length jacket. There was a yard and a half of leftover fabric with it. Many times I was tempted to use it for trim (corduroy passes quite nicely for velvet), but somehow it never seemed quite the right thing to do. And when eventually I needed a tail coat, what could have been better? In less than an hour I cut out the tails and sewed them to the coat. Some years later, when the same singer reappeared, this time needing a 17th-century doublet, I removed the tails and added a peplum.

Button It Up

As any costumer knows, the price of buttons has been steadily climbing, and buttons can add a tidy sum to the total cost of a costume. Since I first began designing costumes, I've been voraciously collecting buttons. Gone are the days when I tossed my clothes without cutting off the buttons. And as far as I'm concerned, you can hardly buy nice buttons anymore, either for ordinary clothes or for costumes, unless you happen to be mad about plastic. The best buttons I've ever had came from a distress merchandise man who gave me a laundry basket full of loose buttons — thousands of them, some mother of pearl, wood bone, and great old underwear buttons.

Large buttons can be used for Renaissance medallions. Spray them with metallic paint and glue on sequins or jewels. Spraying with metallic paint will even work on some kinds of plastic buttons. Spray metal buttons back and forth from silver to gold to get more mileage out of them.

To make your own buttons, cut out pieces of felt (or

any heavy fabric) and glue several layers together. Size them with varnish. Be sure to leave the varnish off the bottom layer so you can sew them on.

Whenever you can, use shank buttons (which have an extension on the back) and pin them on. You can adjust them more easily for a better fit, and you save time when you take them off. (See figure 5.83.)

Figure 5.83 – Shank button

It's Younger than It Looks: Aging an Outfit

Beggars are less than convincing if price tags dangle from their clothing. We expect beggars and some other folk to have dingy, well-worn outfits. But if you must supply your beggars with new garments, here are a few tips for making them appear older than they are.

- Dunk the garment in a shade of dye darker or lighter than the original color.

- Pull threads, creating your own rips and tears. Ripping the garment before you wash it will help fray the seams.

- Stitch on patches, but beware of phony looking patches. Cloth should be a close match and large enough to look as if it were really needed, and the patch should be in a place likely to wear out.

- Wash the garment in your machine with a little fabric bleach, or, for light-colored clothing, with dark colors that will fade and dingy-up the fabric.

- A length of rag or a rope tied around the waist creates a less affluent look, and burlap-like material tied around the feet is always good.

Taking Care of the Elderly: Antique Clothing

Anyone fortunate enough to have access to authentic clothing should care for it properly, for these pieces are treasures that would be difficult to replace. Museums hang their period costumes on very broad, heavily padded, custom-made hangers, or lay them flat in special metal cabinets with lots of narrow drawers. Sometimes the cabinets are even custom made, but they can be found in stock. Ideally there should be one costume per drawer. If more than one costume is stored in a drawer, sheets of non-acidic tissue paper should be placed between them. If the storage facility is made of wood, put non-acidic paper between the costumes and the wood since wood stains clothing. You may substitute muslin for the non-acidic paper. Non-acidic paper and boxes may be ordered from: University Products, Inc. (phone 1-800-628-1921), 517 Main St., P.O. Box 101, Holyoke, MA 01041-0101; or from Light Impressions (phone 1-800-828-6216), 439 Monroe Ave., Rochester, NY 14607.

Padding regular hangers with paper, about an inch in diameter, will help prevent creases in unwanted places. If the garment is heavy, be sure it is adequately supported to prevent damage to shoulders. This is especially true of dresses with heavy skirts. If you can neither hang costumes on padded hangers nor lay them in drawers, roll them in tissue for storage.

Above all, you want to prevent damage from pesky little invaders. Remember that bugs like to eat starch, so always store garments clean and free of starch. Because mothballs are made of chemicals, and dry cleaning is a chemical process, your antiques should never be exposed to either. The experts at the Colorado Springs Pioneers Museum put costumes that are suspected of having moths (moths only eat wool) or other bugs in plastic bags, one costume per bag. They vacuum out the air, seal them with a twist-tie and put the bags in a freezer for 24 hours. Then they take the bag out for 24 hours, and then repeat in the freezer for another 24 hours. After removing a costume from the bag, they vacuum it carefully.

Stains cause chemical reactions which in turn cause fabric to disintegrate, and therefore these stains are not removable — a good reason to be very strict in caring for your antique clothing when worn.

If you must make, add to, or alter your antiques, be sure the fabric is sturdy enough and use a delicate hand stitch. To restore a place that has rotted in your fabric, cover the worn-out spot with cotton net by tacking the net over it inconspicuously. This will help to stabilize and strengthen the weak place. Olive green net seems to blend best, even against reds. (That's what I saw being used at the Denver Art Museum.)

Steaming is the best way to freshen antique clothing. A drapery steamer works wonders, but may be difficult to locate or borrow from your local cleaners. There are now a variety of hand-held steamers available. Their purchase may be a worthwhile investment.

Organizing Sets of Costumes

You started out just making your own costume, or a costume for your child. But you were good at it, and it was fun. And other people liked your costumes. Pretty soon, the drama teacher at the high school heard about your talents and asked you if you'd help with the school play. Now, you're knee deep in the community theater!

There are special challenges to costuming an entire cast. When you're making more than one costume, using ready-made clothes will really be a godsend. If you worry that your ability to design will be minimized, you'll soon discover that your imagination is just as taxed, only in a different way. Recognizing the hidden possibilities, figuring out ways to make a whole lot of unrelated garments into a set of costumes is a fascinating problem. Singling out what will work and discarding what will not takes practice. In some areas there are no short cuts, in others there are many — some of which can even lead to better costuming for less money.

Instead of counting sheep at night, go through the thrift shop racks in your mind. What color, for instance, is dominant? Could you build a set of costumes on it? Do you have other gowns and fabrics to go with it? Or would it be better to start with another color, even though it isn't as prevalent?

To make a group of costumes from the fabrics and ready-made clothes you have collected, start by spreading it all out on the floor, chairs, anywhere. Then, beginning with your pièce de résistance — the gown or fabric you know you absolutely must use — start adding other compatible pieces to the pile. If you are making more than one group, put each pile together the same way, maybe using a color as a starter rather than a special gown or material. Eventually you will have several piles of things that go together. Then you can decide which piles will work best for you.

After you've made your piles and decided what you can use and what to discard, you'll have to decide on what kind of fabric to buy in order to complete each set of costumes. No matter how many times I've done it, buying fabric is an awesome prospect. For one thing, the color you want most usually is the one you won't find. This means you'll have to rethink your color scheme on the wing. So it isn't a good idea to let a color become fixed in your mind (or in the director's, incidentally).

My greatest success in picking fabric has come when I've walked into a store and been instantly caught by a particular piece of material. That first glance is always best. When there's nothing there to catch my eye, I have to plod through everything, and exhausting, "intelligent" decisions must take the place of instinctive ones. Maybe I'd had blue in mind, but the blues I can choose from are a bit off, while the greens are good. Or the color I really want isn't available in a fabric of the right weight — or price. Colors, like everything else, come and go. The same is true of fabric. In '69 there wasn't a scrap of plaid taffeta; six years later, it was everywhere. Maddening, but par for the course.

Don't worry too much about whether a certain shade will look better under the lights. You can't know what the lighting is going to be. Sometimes you get a pleasant surprise, sometimes an unpleasant one. Lighting plans are something that undergo metamorphosis until the opening curtain, and sometimes even after that. If you're lucky, you'll have a lighting man who realizes that too much light reveals too much imperfection (both costumes and sets). If you're unlucky, you'll have one who thinks only in absolutes . . . daylight is bright, night is dark. A good lighting man can be your best friend when it comes to hiding multiple sins.

Count on raw colors to look more raw under stage light. Beautiful colors and fabrics will look more beautiful. Fluorescent lights in stores are a nuisance, so make a daylight test if you can. Stage lighting is closer to daylight than fluorescent. After you've bought a lot of fabric and seen a lot of it on stage, your eye will adjust to fluorescent lighting and you'll be able to predict the result.

If you're starting from scratch, work from the general to the particular. Don't finish one costume at a time. Rather, make them in giant steps: Cut all the gowns out, sew them together, and do another group the same way. Leave the finishing and trimming till the end. That way you have something, trimmed or not, for everyone to put on, and it's just as well not to do the finishing too soon, since you may have some changes in the cast as you go along. It's much easier to trim a set of costumes all at once instead of each one individually. You can get a better idea of how much trim you'll need and how to spread it around. You'll also get a chance to use some of the ideas that may have crept into your mind after you made your original plans.

Costume sewing is not the same as dressmaking. If you're upset by crooked or unfinished seams and other shortcuts, you'll probably be unhappy making costumes. It just isn't practical to spend lots of time on beautiful sewing and finishing. There's never lots of time, or labor, so aiming for perfection only leads to frustration. The law that says "work expands to fill the allotted time" was never truer than when you're making costumes.

Coping with a Chorus

If you're responsible for costuming an entire show, you'll fret about whether you can make the principals look the way you'd like them to. But coping with them will be easy compared to coping with the chorus and the minor leads. Leading characters will be easier to research, and these parts will be cast sooner and be less erratic. For a chorus of 30 or 40, the casting takes longer, the process gets strung out over too long a period of time, and there are always people dropping out without telling anyone, replacements being made without warning, and so on. All the same, getting a chorus decked out was always exciting to me. There's something very satisfying in taking a motley lot of people of all ages and sizes and turning them into a group that looks as if it belongs together.

For a chorus, about four basic colors in various shades and hues is enough. The more you use colors in the same hues, the more stylized your effect. Colors can be close to one another on the spectrum, or mostly earthy or pastel; you can throw in a few bright spots with either, just so your accents are distributed so that they look intentional.

I used to think I had to wait until the casting was done to do the chorus costumes. But as that was terribly hectic when there were a lot of complicated gowns, I finally decided to try doing the chorus ahead of time. Going over past statistics, I realized that for a chorus of 16 women, I'd be safe making two size 16s, four size 14s, four size 12s, four 10s, two 8s. Even though pattern measurements have been adjusted in recent years, I still use a pattern size 12 to make a size 10 dress, and so on up and down the scale. Always sew costumes with the longest stitch on your machine. You'll be so glad you did when you have

111

to rip seams out, and ripping out is inevitable. If you end up with five size 10 women, it's still easier to take in the seams on one of the 12s than to start from scratch again. Remember, though, whenever you can, don't rip out your sewing to correct an error; instead, change tack. If a dress turns out to be too small for a particular member of the chorus, try it on someone else. Or try to incorporate the mistake into the design: If you've made a puff on a Renaissance sleeve lower or higher than the other, add a small puff to even them up, or perhaps use trim to cover up the difference.

A very large or very small person won't fit into the 8-16 range, but then often they need special treatment anyhow. Depending on how the chorus is structured (stylized as in Gilbert and Sullivan, or milling around, etc.), extra large or small people can often be used in ways that are more comfortable for them than making them try to fit into an analogous group. Maybe a very large woman would make a better innkeeper than she would one of the girls. For this you need a cooperative director who is willing to do a little extra thinking. In ballroom scenes, there can always be maids, footmen, guards. (Why is it that when you have a bunch of uniforms size 40 to 42, the director will choose a short, fat size 46 for the job?)

Choruses are always more interesting if they are treated as individuals, and it can solve some costume problems, too, like having to buy ten yards of material to make an enormous gown from scratch that might never be worn again. It can also make problems if your director waits until the last minute to make too many exotic decisions, like suddenly introducing four new guards. It's amazing how often directors leave things like that till the last minute. To them it may be a minor detail; to you it could mean a whole set of new uniforms. It's a good idea to check on what's happening at rehearsals: A scene may get cut, a maid added. Or maybe that coat you thought the male lead would wear is suddenly to be used as a cue, so instead of wearing it, he leaves it on stage and goes about in that shirt you gave him without full sleeves and the vest with the funny-looking back.

When it comes to hemming, trimming, and sometimes even fitting, you can often get help from chorus members if you just ask. If everyone is a volunteer, staff members included, it will be easier to get help, but the outcome will be less organized since people who volunteer to make whole costumes quite naturally want a voice in the result. If you know your volunteers, then you are fairly safe. If you don't, be wary of delegating too much responsibility. I remember a volunteer who waited until the night before dress rehearsal to sew 144 buttons on eight uniforms, and instead of sewing that evening, she went to the hospital. Somehow volunteers very seldom feel it is their job to get someone to do their work if they can't. They just return the unfinished costumes to the costumer.

White Ties and Gloves

White ties are getting very hard to find second hand, so you'll probably have to make them. Instead of a clip, you can use a piece of elastic that goes around the back of the neck to keep them on. For earlier ties, you'll have to make a tie out of a strip of soft, white fabric. Make it about 5" wide and 65"-70" long. Fold it to 2½" wide, sew it, and turn it to the right side.

White gloves for men are practically nonexistent now (second hand, that is) except at military surplus stores where they are relatively expensive. A dollar a pair adds up when you're working with a chorus of 15 or 20 men, but for an opera such as *Masked Ball* they are a wonderful touch if you can afford them. Principals often don't want to be bothered with gloves, so don't go to great lengths to provide them unless you've a specific request.

Making a Face

As a costumer, you may be called upon to assist with — or assume complete responsibility for — make-up from time to time. Check with your librarian for the best references.

When I first started doing make-up, I used to experiment with different shades of make-up on the chorus. I have never found any that I liked better than Stein's Tan Blush, Russet, Suntan, and Egyptian. All of these shades have lots of red in them. They are also quite dark, yet Suntan and Egyptian are the ones I use most often. For a long time I thought needing so much red might have something to do with the lights in our theater. When I went to work in more modern theaters, I tried more conventional shades, like Max Factor's Tan No. 2, but they looked no better. For a good Broadway look, I think the dark shades with red are better. A helpful hint: Ammonia rubbed on shirt collars before washing helps remove make-up.

Another trademark of the unprofessional is neglected hair, and this I have seen in cities as big as Denver. If there is no one in your company who can research hairdos and help the cast achieve some reasonable facsimile, then get a hairdresser who can. Hairdressers are just as attracted to show business as other people; often you can get one to donate his or her services for a nice mention in the program. If not, you can probably find someone who will at least get you on the right track for a small fee.

Something to watch out for is too much authenticity. Attractiveness is as much fashion as anything. Bright scarlet lips look as wrong on stage as off when contemporary fashion dictates pale. Entire productions — costumes, sets, direction — get dated. Just look at pictures of yesterday's opera singers, or look at an old movie on TV. Movies made now about the '30s do not look like movies made during the '30s. What dates them is that they do not reflect our idea of what is appealing now, and our eyes can't make the adjustment. A dyed-in-the-wool advo-

114

cate of authenticity might claim that this is no excuse for taking liberties, and I'd agree if pleasing the audience were not a legitimate concern.

Chapter 6
THE PLAY'S THE THING

The Costume Parade

A costume parade is supposed to be of benefit to all concerned. And, to be sure, if you can get your cast to assemble in costume several days prior to the dress rehearsal for an inspection, everyone, yourself included, will have a much better idea, much sooner, of what's been happening in the costume department. When you have doubts about what you've done in some areas, the suspense of waiting until the dress rehearsal to find out if your doubts are justified can be almost unbearable, especially as you know you'll be up all night if you bungled. After the dress rehearsal there is so little time to make amends. While for a costumer a costume parade may be a nightmare, it does turn the dress rehearsal into almost a lark. For the director, a costume parade should also relieve the pressure, since he is able to give the costumes his undivided attention, something he couldn't possibly do at a dress rehearsal. However, there are directors who prefer not to be bothered by what they consider just one more imposition on their time, and there are many people in casts who feel the same way. For the cast, it does mean a lot of boring standing around waiting for turns. With a cast of 40 or 50, a costume parade can last three hours.

Another disadvantage is that even if you are able to have the parade on the stage, there probably won't be any lights. Not even work lights, maybe, because the set people will be too busy this late in the game to bother. I had designed a lot of costumes before I was blessed with my first costume parade. No amount of experience would have been enough to console me when I first saw a whole cast in costumes without hairdos, bare-faced, and without any lights. They were pathetic. All in all, even though I am certainly one for getting as much put in order as far ahead as possible, I think I prefer having several dress rehearsals instead of a costume parade. While the lights probably wouldn't be set correctly, they would at least be on, the stage crew wouldn't be hammering two feet behind the apron, and, above all, you can see how the costumes work in the actual situation.

The problem that develops with early dress rehearsals is that the stage business will still be incomplete, and so a run-through also ends up being incomplete, which means there might be some costumes you aren't able to see, some fast changes that don't get practiced. Here again, you are at the mercy of your director. A good director will have his stage business far enough along so that the show can be run through in an evening's time.

However, if your director feels that a costume parade is a must, then you should keep two things in mind. The first is that other people tend to get the idea that a costume parade is some sort of show, and therefore they will attend if you let them. A costume parade is a technical rehearsal, and like any other technical rehearsal it should be attended only by the people who are involved. Second, don't let anyone in your publicity department send in someone from a TV station or newspaper. This is no time for movies or photographs. Arrange them some other time when you can have nothing else on your mind. I remember a singer who had been in for his fitting, and though he complained that his costume didn't work as well as a previous one he'd once had (his coat and shirt had to come off on-stage), he decided, before leaving that day, that he could cope. At the costume parade, in front of a TV camera, he had a very strange reversal. Suddenly nothing was right, and all he could do was hitch it here and hike it there, complaining loudly, putting on a one-man show. As it turned out, after the camera episode, he never said another word and wore the costume as it was. Performers do funny things in costume parades when they are unhappy. I can still see in my mind a 6'2" man hopping around like an enormous jack rabbit because he didn't like his boots and wanted to be sure everyone saw he couldn't walk naturally in them. Of course, there are also the ones who would sooner be strangled by a sword belt than complain in front of a lot of people.

As to the mechanics of a costume parade, plan to bring the principals through first, then bring the chorus on in a group. Plan to have two helpers, one to get people into their costumes, another to take notes. You will find it next to impossible to both confer with the director about problems and at the same time be making notes of the corrections. Very important is making note of how much too big or too small, too long or too short, a costume is. Then you can go ahead and make the changes without having to arrange and take time for another fitting.

While the Show Goes On

The functions of Wardrobe include making the final costume adjustments and seeing that during the run of the show the costumes are clean, pressed and repaired. While it can be, as in colleges and schools, that costumes are also made in the same place, costumes are usually made somewhere else: a workshop or costume company. The amount of work involved in the final adjustments depends on how conscientiously the costume company did its job. Under normal circumstances all that should be required of Wardrobe is a few nips and tucks and the fast-change adjustments. If a director makes some dramatic last minute changes, Wardrobe will be rushed. If someone in the cast gets sick and has to be replaced by an actor of a different size, Wardrobe will be working overtime. It has happened that a different tenor has sung each of three acts in an opera. In this case, comfort yourself by recalling the photos you've seen in costume books of real people in days past and how both fitting and maintenance fell far short of what they do now.

My first Wardrobe job was coincidental: The wardrobe mistress for *The Odd Couple* in Central City, Colorado, had to leave before the play finished its run. I would have no problems, I was told, since the costumes were just ordinary clothes. And so it turned out that what I did was mostly washing, a bit of ironing, maybe sewing on a button. During one show I would wash the alternate set of shirts so that they would be ready for the next. When a scene change had to be accomplished in a matter of seconds, I had to rush out and lay a coat on the back of a chair so that it would be there when the lights went on. Occasionally there would be something extra, like Phil Foster bringing his socks in to be thrown in the washing machine, someone else with a seersucker robe to add to my light load. Both were welcome diversions, and it seemed to me quite silly that the union had rules about what Wardrobe is supposed to do and not do.

My second Wardrobe job, assistant wardrobe mistress during an opera season again in Central City, was completely different. Loads of people coming in and going out, three weeks of sewing all day and half the night (in the lovely month of June during which it rained continuously, lowering the temperature to 42 degrees in Wardrobe where the only heat came from the dryer). It was during this siege that I began to catch a glimpse of why the union had strict rules about the division of labor and personal favors. Once the performance began, the sewing let up, but the washing began, and there was practically never a time when there weren't shirts hanging in a row waiting to be ironed.

The wardrobe master was a man named Herbert Flyer. He was a master of courtesy and consideration. Always nice to everyone, he was a marvel at telling the people who worked in Wardrobe exactly what he wanted, which saved endless time and was easy on the nerves. I think of him often when I'm telling someone about a costume alteration that has to be done; most especially when I hear myself saying something like, "Oh, make it a couple of inches or so smaller." Herb would never have allowed himself such leeway. Because he tried so hard to satisfy the performers, they were extremely fond of him and he made Wardrobe, besides everything else, a very sociable port in the storm.

A third and totally different experience was being wardrobe mistress for *Cactus Flower*. Because the company was beginning its 14-month national run in Central City and the costumes had not yet been worn, a wardrobe person came out from New York to solve the major wardrobe problems. This very talkative, friendly woman had spent her entire life in Wardrobes, and she now materialized as a sort of professional granny. Her pocketbook, about the size of a carpetbag, was loaded with remedies ranging from candy to aspirin, and along with these were a host of other items to be used rather than eaten, like snaps, garters, scissors, hairpins. Within a couple of days she became so enamored of Central City that she decided it would be nice to stay for the run of the play. In order to accomplish this, she also decided that the ingénue should have me for a dresser, instead of my taking over Wardrobe when she went back to New York. One look at the row of shoes I would have had to keep in order was enough to make me very glad the company did not have the money to spend on another dresser. *Cactus Flower* is a terrible show for a dresser; a costume change for every scene, and about a dozen scenes. I believe it was this wardrobe mistress who told me that retired strippers often ended up in Wardrobe, but that now, since working in Wardrobe has grown more respectable (as has being a performer), it is more likely to be the daughter of a wardrobe mistress who has the job. The profession is crowded now; unions are strong and in some states it's a long time before you can join.

The costumes for *Cactus Flower* had to be kept in super-perfect condition. In real life, Hugh O'Brien is known for his natty clothes. In the theater he stays in character. The first shirts I ironed for him were brought back and my attention was called to a wrinkle or two in the collar. To get a collar smooth, he told me, you have to iron the underside first. Try it; it works.

Another of my *Cactus Flower* jobs was getting an actor out of a suit and into a tuxedo, again crossing union lines, since wardrobe mistresses are not supposed to be dressers. Theater companies, on the whole, are run along much more formal lines than opera companies, mostly, I think, because the lack of funds forces opera companies into a more casual attitude. But even so, it was while working for *Cactus Flower* that I really saw why the unions set strict guidelines. Ridiculous though they may seem in many cases, there are always a few people who can't resist slipping in with mending to be done on their personal clothes, pants to be shortened, something to launder, and usually the wardrobe personnel are loath to refuse.

There is royalty in the dressing rooms. There is also a decided lack of class. The former is much more often the rule. Some performers are so secure they will work with anything. Others indulge in compulsive fussing, and, of course, it is the fussers who stand out. The first one I think of began by demanding a major alteration upon the back of a coat designed and made especially for him by a major costume company. He then became obsessed with the elastics that went under the sole of his foot to keep his pants taut. One would be too tight one day, the next day it would be too loose. The day after that it was tight again. The pants kept coming back; we accepted them, laid them aside, presented them again upon request. Finally he decided he needed a quarter inch added to the heel of one of his boots. But, we said, there is no shoe repair in Central City. Well, he wouldn't sing if something wasn't done. So I drove to various neighboring towns, finally getting the boot done after driving 60 miles.

The second most temperamental fusser I remember was the kind of person who was upset by the slightest deviation from the most conventional, orthodox costume. "Do I have to wear that?" he'd fume. "Well, I don't mean to make trouble, but isn't it awfully long?" and so on, with most every detail that wasn't exactly what he was used to. He was so impossible, he could reduce a dresser to tears. More than plain nastiness, it was nerves. Once he got into a production, he was almost human.

Sometimes not giving a performer enough attention

makes problems. I recall a baritone storming in on us, his costume half on, some of it being dragged and very nearly thrown at us — and no wonder, since we'd left him to cope with one of those costumes that is worse than a puzzle to get into, and the crowning blow was a sash that he could hardly be expected to wind into by himself.

When the costumes fit and are becoming, when all the accessories work out, costuming is exhilarating. But inevitably, there will be less glorious times. While a production may have been designed with a particular artist in mind, the princial roles will be taken by many other artists during the production's lifetime. Designing and constructing costumes from a set of measurements and maybe a glamorized head-and-shoulders photo leaves something to be desired, namely the body itself. When created from a distance, as costumes often are, whether by one of the best-known costume companies or the most lowly, there will occasionally be unbecoming results.

Costume Changes and Dressers

Though I've never actually worked as a dresser, I've done enough dressing to admire them. A dressing room is usually a pretty small place to be cooped up in with another person. It can be not too different from being caged with a large, friendly, panting St. Bernard. Or it can be like having a flock of birds locked in a closet. Besides having to be friendly, courteous, and patient, you have to have your wits about you. You can't forget what's supposed to be laid out, where, when or how. Changes of costume can happen in all sorts of backstage cubbyholes, and a dresser has to be wherever this is with all the right things at the right time. A few moments later simply won't do. Sometimes performers will double-check you themselves, if they've a few minutes off-stage, and sometimes they'll get someone else to do it.

One of the first things you look for when you're reading a play is how many changes are indicated for each member of the cast. At the New York State Opera there has been the tradition of keeping everyone in the same costume all the way through regardless of how the scenes change, and many companies do the same. Though I've always felt costume changes help to express the passage of time, the saving of money and work hours is probably a more important consideration. This is something you should think about and decide with your director before you start working. My own opinion is that spoiling illusion is never a good idea; if by changing costumes you help preserve it, then you should change costumes. Costume changes are also a source of enjoyment and interest to the audience. If you can't find the time or money required, then it might be better to do a less complicated show.

In small companies, the designer, the wardrobe mistress and the dressers are all likely to be the same person. While I always enjoyed being around the dressing rooms to see how things were going, I'd do just about anything not to dress the principals for the first dress rehearsal. In the heat of such a trying time, it's much better to have a dresser for whom the costumes are less personal.

Performers react in different ways to services obtained from Wardrobe. Some take any amount for granted, others are grateful for the least bit of help. Dressers are apt to receive tips (the bigger the star, the more likely). Wardrobe as a whole occasionally receives presents like something good to eat or drink. Wardrobe supervisors may receive either or both. No doubt, what is the appropriate thing to do is often perplexing to performers, since wardrobe personnel runs a rather wide gamut: You might be having your pants sewn up by a former stripper or maybe by a college girl!

When a new set of costumes is received by a professional company, one of the first things Wardrobe does is make alterations for the fast changes. For Hugh O'Brien in *Cactus Flower* we cut off the cuffs on his shirts and sewed them into his jacket sleeves so that he didn't have to take time to unbutton them. Then there was Velcro in place of the fastenings on his dentist's jackets, and I think there were some snaps in place of buttons on a vest.

One thing you should be sure of is a chance to rehearse the fast change. Hopefully, you will have two dress rehearsals: You need the first just to find out what is going to fly off and how, and who's going to do what and when. Often the performer can do a particular job better than you, or the singer can be doing one thing while you do another. Unless this is planned, you can also get in each other's way. Funny things have a way of happening under pressure. Like characters who've been unconcerned and who you can hardly get to try a costume on during rehearsals will suddenly be ripping things off, popping buttons, busting zippers. Not much fun for you the next day. For some shows more than one person, or a person on each side of the stage, will be needed, and it could be that you need to construct some measure of privacy, if the change involves changing undergarments or some such in front of stagehands. Someone to hold a blanket up is a help. Wearing one costume under another is sometimes a way, but it's tricky unless the second costume is much skimpier than the first.

The on-stage change is a whole different bag. To accomplish this, as often as not there will suddenly be some maids or companions thrown in, people not already in the show, or people who, even if they are in the show, still need another costume to be suitably dressed for the dressing scene they are going to assist with. And suddenly you may need some underwear you hadn't planned on. In a *Romeo and Juliet* I once costumed, the director was determined not to have Juliet go behind a screen to put on her wedding dress. A couple of "companions" were selected to hold up a robe in front of her. Not a bad idea, except the robe was not enough for total concealment, and a period slip was the only solution. It is not a good idea to depend on the director to think about things like this ahead of time.

EPILOGUE:
BEHIND THE SCENES

No matter how many productions you manage to survive, it's always exciting to hear new voices, to meet new personalities. My first experience as a costume designer involved a Metropolitan soprano who, of course, was used to the best. As a designer, the only time I'm nervous is between meeting the artist and getting the costumes on. During those moments all my self-assurance drains away and I'm ready to throw my costumes into the trash. In the fitting room this particular soprano took off her dress, and before I could hand her her first costume, she put on a little white blouse. Hm. But then, when she tried on the costume, she exclaimed, "Why, it's brand new!" The blouse was to protect her from what she expected would be dirty, second-hand or rented dresses. Besides the newness, the colors pleased her, and we got them to fit well, too. I have often thought how lucky I was to have had this extremely nice person for my first costume job. This soprano, by the way, also was thoughtful enough to bring her own black stockings and appropriate shoes. I say "thoughtful," but it also seems to me that a singer who is going to be traveling around would consider it a kindness to herself to possess such basic things as white and black tights that fit and a pair of small-heeled black shoes that are comfortable. The union specifies that shoes should be new, but this is one rule that by necessity is overlooked, since it isn't always possible to buy the kind of shoes you want, and for a small company to have shoes custom made for a one- or two-night stand is extravagant.

A few years of working with costumes taught me not to be surprised that one cuff on a jacket might look an inch shorter than the other because the lengths of everyone's arms are not the same. Nor does it surprise me that interpretations vary: The shabby clothes I like to see worn when the furniture is being burned for warmth in

Boheme may not always be acceptable. Some children think it's more fun to wear pretty dresses than to be street urchins, and if you don't want to hear a lot of distressed small voices, children should be prepared for their roles ahead of time.

It wasn't surprising when a good-natured baritone like Chet Ludgin, who admitted he was a big, tall man and not easily fitted, thought to bring his own cowboy hat, his own boots and jeans to help with his costumes for *Suzannah*. And I learned to expect that my favorite tenor, Gene Bullard, would hunt around in his suitcase for a good-looking belt or whatever other accessory he could provide.

Providing little courtesies will usually make a temperamental performer much more cooperative. I often remind myself that though it may be a lark to dress up occasionally and assume a new identity, to make a life of being measured and fitted, dabbed and combed, to be constantly controlled by a situation someone else made up and have to follow a beat set by another, all the while being dependent on two little muscles called vocal chords, well, a singer is in some ways a rare phenomenon. For a good beginning, have someone meet your performer's plane and take him or her to his or her hotel. Every company should have volunteers who will make the artist feel he is being looked after: Is everything satisfactory with the room? Does he need anything from local stores that he can't locate on his own? If time permits, is someone available to show him local sights?

It's glamorous to envision beautiful sopranos and voluptuous mezzos, sensual tenors and handsome baritones relaxing in fancy hotels and dining on lobsters and ribs in exotic places, and, no doubt for some there are times of plenty; but more likely the incoming cast will be holed up in budget accommodations, roughing out makeshift meals on a cooking unit if they can, and after late rehearsals, the only places still open will be franchise, fast-food restaurants.

The theater is a microcosm through which fans roam,

some looking to be thrilled by high notes, others searching for perfect productions. Great voices and great performers are not always heard or seen in great productions; less great productions don't always have less-than-great voices or performers. Few productions ever have perfect stars and choruses, perfect costumes and sets. But I think that's exactly what keeps it so interesting . . . always trying to do better for the performers, the director, the producer and the audience. A good show, thanks to a great team effort, is its own wonderful reward.

GLOSSARY

Cowl Tube that drapes and folds around the neck above a garment's neckline. *See figure 2.9 page 16.*

Cravat Scarf for a man's neck, usually white. *See reference page 44.*

Eton collar Large, stiff, turnover collar. *See figure 2.58 page 71.*

Fichu Triangular scarf, often white, usually a lightweight fabric, that was draped over the shoulders with the ends fastened in front to fill in a low neckline. *See figure 2.24 page 29.*

Gusset Diamond-shaped piece of material, about 6" x 4" depending on how much extra room you need under the arm. You place the gusset at the point where the underarm seam meets the undersleeve seam. *See reference page 104.*

Homespun Loosely woven fabric, usually woolen, usually on the heavy side. *See reference on page 9.*

Jabot Small neckpiece, sometimes pleated, sometimes ruffled or trimmed with lace to cover the front of a man's neck; usually white. See figure 2.29 (D) page 35.

Knickers Loose-fitting short pants gathered just below the knee. Fuller than knee-breeches. *See figure 2.30 page 37.*

Mantle Big piece of fabric that is draped over other clothing. *See figure 2.7 page 15.*

Peplum Short skirt attached to the waist of a blouse; sometimes full, sometimes narrow. *See figures 2.46 and 3.69 (pages 55 and 84 respectively).*

Pinafore Like an apron that has an upper front and straps over the shoulders; often ruffled. *See figure 2.59 page 72.*

Puttees Leather or cloth covering the leg from the ankle to under the knee. *See figure 3.72 page 87.*

Shank buttons	Buttons that have a projection on the back by which the button is sewn to the fabric. *See figure 5.83 page 106.*
Stand	The part of a collar on a man's shirt that makes the collar stand up. *See figure 2.52 page 63.*
Stock	Same as jabot. *See figure 2.29 (D) page 35.*
Tabard	Short, sleeveless tunic. *See figure 2.19 page 24.*
Windsor tie	Broad necktie, usually tied in a loose bow. *See figure 2.58 page 71.*

ABOUT THE AUTHOR

Photo: Eileene Philpot

Musician, designer, painter, writer — these talents and proficiences mark Shirley Dearing as a true "Renaissance Woman." They comprise the perfect blend of skills to qualify her as an authority for a book about practical costume-making.

Following her degrees in music from Barnard College of Columbia University, New York and art from the University of Colorado, Colorado Springs, Shirley moved into the professional world of the fine arts. She sang and designed opera costumes for various Colorado opera companies. Her expertise in designing led to a companion career as a painter. Her works have appeared in many national exhibitions and juried art shows.

Her work as a costume designer has expanded beyond the world of opera to stage shows and museum work.

Shirley's husband of 34 years is an architect. Together they enjoy adventure travel and the challenge of new languages. She is beginning her sixth year of studying French.

Busy as she is, no one will venture a prediction about what new world she may choose next to conquer.

*Another
helpful
costuming book
from
Meriwether
Publishing . . .*

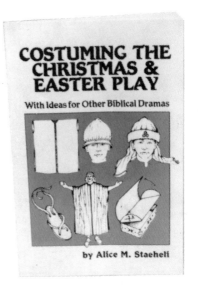

COSTUMING THE CHRISTMAS & EASTER PLAY

by ALICE M. STAEHELI

Packed with photos and detailed illustrations, this exceptionally helpful book gives practical ideas and information on how you can costume almost any type of religious play on a limited budget. Costume designs are based on the authentic clothing styles of the period, but they're simplified to give you more time for important things like rehearsals. You'll also find drawings, photos, detailed dimensions and many suggestions about props, storage and handling of costumes. With this book, you'll find your dramatic productions take on a more professional look. This paperback book is available at bookstores or from Meriwether Publishing Ltd.

Paperback Book (96 pages)   ISBN #0-916260-09-7

*A completely
new way
to use the
open stage!*

SELF-SUPPORTING
SCENERY

by JAMES HULL MILLER

Free-standing scenery creates its own theatre — compact, economical and flexible. It marches right onto any stage platform, into the classroom, the recreation hall and the garden theatre. This book tells how to construct it. Includes 120 pages and over 175 drawings. Covers tools, materials, designs and craft. An excellent reference book. Written by a leading designer in the field. This book is available at bookstores or from Meriwether Publishing Ltd.

Paperback Book (120 pages)   ISBN #0-916260-15-1

ORDER FORM

TM

MERIWETHER PUBLISHING LTD.
P.O. BOX 7710
COLORADO SPRINGS, CO 80933
TELEPHONE: (719) 594-4422

Please send me the following books:

_____**Elegantly Frugal Costumes #TT-B125**   **$10.95**
by Shirley Dearing
A do-it-yourself costume maker's guide

_____**Costuming the Christmas and Easter Play #TT-B180** **$7.95**
by Alice M. Staeheli
How to costume any religious play

_____**The Theatre and You #TT-B115**   **$14.95**
by Marsh Cassady
An introductory text on all aspects of theatre

_____**Small Stage Sets on Tour #TT-B102**   **$9.95**
by James Hull Miller
A practical guide to portable stage sets

_____**Self-Supporting Scenery #TT-B105**   **$9.95**
by James Hull Miller
A scenic workbook for the open stage

_____**The Scenebook for Actors #TT-B177**   **$14.95**
by Norman Bert
Great monologs and dialogs for auditions

_____**Theatre Alive! #TT-B178**   **$24.95**
by Norman Bert
An introductory anthology of world drama

I understand that I may return any book
for a full refund if not satisfied.

NAME: _____

ORGANIZATION NAME: _____

ADDRESS: _____

CITY: _____ STATE: _____ ZIP: _____

PHONE: _____

☐ **Check Enclosed**
☐ **Visa or Master Card #**_____

Signature: _____ *Expiration*
                                        Date: _____
(required for Visa/Mastercard orders)

COLORADO RESIDENTS: Please add 3% sales tax.
SHIPPING: Include $1.50 for the first book and 50¢ for each additional book ordered.

☐ *Please send me a copy of your complete catalog of books and plays.*